Reflections on Quality in 10½ Columns

A Thought-Provoking View on Quality,
Sustainability, Football and
Other Important Things

Willy Vandenbrande

Reflections on Quality in 10½ Columns

A Thought-Provoking View on Quality,
Sustainability, Football and
Other Important Things

© 2023 Willy Vandenbrande

willy@qsconsult.be

Cover design and pictures: © Els Wallaert

Based on the winning picture of the Photographic International Contest 'Quality Pictures,' Porto, November 9, 2023.

ISBN: 978-1-907925-73-3 (Hardback)

ISBN: 978-1-907925-72-6 (Paperback)

ISBN: 978-1-907925-71-9 (e-Book)

MAKEWAY PUBLISHING AND PRINTING

makeway
...enabling desired results

www.makewaybooks.com

Dedicated to my mother, Jacqueline Van Ronselé, housewife, and my father, Abel Vandenbrande, labourer.

TABLE OF CONTENTS

INTRODUCTION

After a webinar I gave for CQI (Chartered Quality Institute, UK), I got a really nice comment on LinkedIn. A lady mentioned that my voice resembled Sean Connery's, the ultimate James Bond. Being nothing like Sean Connery, I was obviously very flattered.

Looking at her profile, I noticed something about the books she had written, and the editing business she apparently was in. So, I thanked her for the kind reaction, and asked if she had any tips for me on how to get a book published.

Her reaction was quite straightforward and simple: *"There are already too many books."*

That was a rather sobering sentence for a would-be published writer, but undoubtedly true; it makes one wonder why people keep writing. Why add more books when there is an already way too high stack of uselessness? I figured there was probably only one answer: *arrogance*. Most authors probably agree that there are already too many books, but not like the one he or she is writing.

After some thirty-five years working within quality management, I wondered if there had been anything I had learned from that period that could be of value to current and future quality professionals, managers, and maybe, even the public at large. Being no less arrogant than the next guy, I decided that my view on quality could add something useful to the extensive existing literature on the topic, so I continued writing; it is now a published book.

This is not a '*How to*' book with quality tools or a cookbook on what one should do to become a successful quality leader. It does not have the ambition to be academic either. It is just a series of reflections on various aspects of quality, leadership and life, aimed to make the reader think and reflect on the stories.

Like in all aspects of business, we have some fundamental truths in quality. This book challenges some of them, and as a result, will sometimes conflict with the teachings of our gurus. I do not think it is wise to follow a guru, not in real life or in quality. There really is no challenge in being a follower, so I go with Immanuel Kant when he said "*Sapere Aude*" or "*Dare to Know*," or translated somewhat more freely into "*Dare to Think*," the tagline of my alma mater, the University of Ghent, Belgium.

One thing I have experienced in these thirty-five years is that you learn from mistakes; in fact, all true learning comes from trying things and understanding what works and what does not. In business literature, it is not common to talk about failures; it is much more popular to boast about successes.

But success stories tend to be rather boring and not always trustworthy, so in this book, not many heroes are presented. In the quality world, like in the real world, people try to make the best of things and regularly fail. That is life, there is no shame in it; it is an opportunity for learning.

The title of this book is inspired by the wonderful novel, "*A History of the World in 10½ Chapters*" by Julian Barnes. I am a great admirer of Mr Barnes, and I very much envy his brilliant writing. Because beauty is so important in quality, I have worked very hard to make this book enjoyable to read, and hopefully also interesting for people who are not in the quality field or business.

As the customer is the only and ultimate judge of quality, it will be up to you, dear reader, to evaluate if I have succeeded in this ambitious undertaking. Do let me know what your thoughts are.

Willy Vandenbrande
December 2023

COLUMN 1
ON BEAUTY

A Thing of Beauty is a Joy Forever
John Keats

In 1999, we travelled through Namibia, camping out for three weeks. If you are interested in nature, put Namibia on your travel list; the country is of an unearthly beauty.

One evening, in front of our tent and under an awesome star-filled sky, we mapped out the trip for the following day. In order to save travelling miles, we decided to take a shortcut, driving through some hills instead of around them. In hindsight, I have to admit this was not a good idea and I would advise no one to do that in Namibia. Saving travel miles rarely saves travelling time.

On the other hand, choosing not to travel the paved path (although that in itself is a rarity in Namibia), brings you to special places and special encounters. In this case, in the middle of nowhere, we crossed a small village. Small as in less than twenty houses, so probably just a couple of families living there. The first thing we saw was an old and rusty advertising signboard for Coca Cola. In this globalised world, there is clearly no escaping from adverts and marketing, no matter how far you drive.

The second view was of a man sitting on a chair looking out at his garden right in front of his house, where red flowers were blooming. It was a beautiful sight. Note that these are poor people living in a dry country with barely fertile soil, to say the least. On that spot, he could have planted any edible plant or fruit, but he had decided on red flowers, which have no use other than to be beautiful and to make life a little more bearable and enjoyable.

> *The scene exemplified the absolute essence of quality, what ought to be our true goal: making life more enjoyable for all.*

That is not what we were taught when entering the quality profession. One of the first things I learned in quality management is that quality is not equal to value. In other words, any product can be quality, regardless of its intrinsic characteristics. Quality has to be seen as value for money or fitness for use, fulfilling specifications and expectations, and delivering what was promised.

So in a customer/supplier relationship, and within this line of thinking, quality represents an economic characteristic based on an objective weighing of price versus value.

At a conference in the United States of America, I had dinner with a Canadian friend. She was not a quality professional, but like most people, she was very interested in quality for her business, which was in the tourist industry with a focus on luxury cruises.

We went to a nice steakhouse, and as we had dessert, I talked about quality and the basic fact that absolute value had nothing to do with the attainment of quality. I illustrated this by saying that a hamburger restaurant, like the McDonald's across the street, could just as well be called a quality restaurant as the steakhouse we were seated in.

She looked at me as if I had totally gone mad, and talking absolute nonsense!

I can imagine that this is shocking when you see it happening to a friend. That fundamental point on total quality management, to her, was outright ridiculous! I tried to explain what I meant by using all my quality management knowledge and my limited convincing powers. Eventually, she changed her mind about me going totally mad, but not on my quality statement; to her, that was still complete nonsense.

It was an important moment in my development in quality management, and it changed some of my ideas about quality. It probably could be called an '*Aha*' moment!

I have had many other such moments since, and they have made me doubt several fundamental ideas and absolute truths you often hear in the quality management world. For one, it made me realise that quality professionals see quality differently than normal people. Intrinsic quality does matter!

Recently, in the area where I live, several shops have opened, and offering a wide variety of products at very low prices. Companies like Primark and Action are examples in Belgium, but I am sure similar brands exist worldwide. They are successful businesses that attract a large group of customers. From an economic point of view, you could say they are high-quality organisations. In fact, for many people with difficulty in stretching their pay cheques to the end of the month, they are an extremely valuable and highly essential alternative.

However, there is a lot of criticism about these shops, also from a quality perspective. People are saying that these shops sell cheap junk, and in so doing, they drive out local shops offering products of much higher intrinsic quality. Sometimes, poor people are even criticised for going to these shops, because in a way, they contribute to the decline of local industry. We live in a strange world, where the general line of thinking seems to be that there would be no poverty if there were no poor people, so it is clear who is to blame.

Anyway, the shops I mentioned above do not hide the fact that they sell cheap stuff, and they are not ashamed of it either; rather, it is actually their most important advertisement. However, many companies dislike being associated with cheap products.

An IKEA vice president once gave a presentation where he asked the audience what came to mind when they thought about IKEA. One of the first words shouted out was 'cheap.' The speaker immediately corrected the daring attendant and made it clear that IKEA is not cheap; it offers value for money to the customer. The audience chuckled a little as they felt the same negative connotation to the word, cheap, as the speaker did. But then those who attend quality conferences do not need to go to Primark or Action, not even at the end of the month.

People buying products at these shops are very pleased they exist. But make no mistake: they rarely refer to their purchases as quality products.

Fitness for use at a payable price does not create a feeling of quality.

It is just like people who enjoy a hamburger every now and then would not go to a McDonalds for a special occasion or to have a 'quality' meal. If need be, they would save up until they have enough money to select a slightly fancier place for their family feast.

In a business-to-consumer world, the economic definition of quality is what the producer sees, but the customer judges quality as an intrinsic feature, buying economic quality and being happy with it, but not truly seeing or feeling it as quality.

What about the other end, the really expensive things? How do they relate to quality? Let us take luxury cars as an example.

I have to admit that I am not a car fanatic. To illustrate, two colleagues were vividly talking about a Testarossa, and it took me some minutes before I realised they were talking about a car that turned out to be an iconic Ferrari. Not knowing much about cars, I do know Porsche, so I looked at their website to see what characteristics this luxury brand promotes.

When I checked, the Porsche 911 Carrera S was marketed for €146,196.77 as a starting price. I like the *196.77* at the end; you would think, at that price level, they might as well have rounded it. The first key thing mentioned in its advertisement was a 331 kilowatt (kW) engine that can take the car to accelerate from 0 to 100 (one hundred) kilometres per hour (km/h) in 3.7 seconds. The maximum speed (on circuit) was announced to be 308 km/h. This all appears very impressive, but is this fit for use?

In Belgium, the chances of ever being able to accelerate from 0 to 100 km/h are limited, to say the least, let alone doing it in a time of 3.7 seconds! As the allowable maximum speed on the highway is 120 km/h, you could drive 188 km/h faster with this car. Unfortunately, not on the road, but, as advertised, *'on circuit.'* I liked this addition to the top speed on the website, but also wondered how many Porsche owners would ever drive on a circuit.

So, here you have a ridiculously over-dimensioned engine with characteristics that are either useless or illegal. But then, maybe the car has other interesting characteristics: perhaps it has space for a large family, a trunk volume that allows you to take junk to the recycling park, a very low fuel consumption, a minimal CO_2 exhaust, so perhaps it contributes to the fight against global warming? Not really.

In fact, if fitness for use were the decisive quality characteristic, no one would ever buy a Porsche 911 Carrera S.

Yet, just like IKEA and the price discounters referred to earlier, Porsche is a very successful company. People buy a Porsche because of the brand's reputation, the status it provides, the possibility of feeling like Formula One drivers, such as Lewis Hamilton or Max Verstappen, and of course, because they can afford it! Or perhaps, most of all, because it is a beautiful car. That is something IKEA and Porsche have in common: they make beautiful products of very different intrinsic value, and it is the beauty and styling that attract people.

When I started out as an independent consultant, I had to buy a car. Being in quality management, I decided to use a quality tool to come up with the *objective-data-based-best-buy*. Naturally, I looked for a car of a certain style and within a certain price range. After some pre-selection, I ended up with a shortlist of five models to evaluate. I created an Excel table with the various characteristics of the different cars. I used a scoring system to combine the importance of a requirement with the fulfilment of that requirement by the cars in the study. After this lengthy process, I came up with a final score allowing me to compare the cars in an objective, data-supported way. It turned out to be an utterly useless exercise!

The conclusion of all that work was that cars within a similar segment are technically very similar. Of course, the cars recorded different scores on varied characteristics, but on the balance, they ended up with results that were almost identical. In hindsight, this should not have surprised me, as many key components in various car brands come from the same manufacturer, so technically, they are bound to be similar.

Engineers often think that most people – like they do – go wild on technical details. I have to disappoint them; many more people tend to go wild on beauty rather than on hidden technology. Even I, as an engineer, ended up selecting and buying the car that I found to be the most attractive.

As a tip for developers: it is equally expensive to put an ugly product on the market as it is to create a beautiful one, so there is no point in developing ugly products.

So, quality is a complex mix of fitness for use, intrinsic value, and beauty.

In addition, there is a second lesson I learned early on about quality management: no matter what product you put on the market, regardless of what its value may be or its beauty, you will have to produce it in such a way that you can sell it profitably.

The main contribution of quality to the long term financial sustainability of an organisation lies in the quality of the processes that are used to generate the product, whether it is a Porsche 911 Carrera S or a Billy closet. In relation to the foregoing paragraph, it is equally expensive to produce a bad product as it is to manufacture a good one, so there is absolutely no point in producing bad products.

This is the large knowledge area that I would call technical quality, containing a range of quality tools and methods. There is no way you can overestimate the importance of it. As I already mentioned in the Introduction, this is not a book on quality techniques, because there is already an abundance of excellent literature on this subject. Invariably, it does not mean that I do not find this valuable, on the contrary.

Quality management has made a huge contribution in making organisations more efficient, of higher quality, with lower waste, and overall, more competitive.

In relation to the cost, quality and speed triangle, quality management has been the major factor in improving all three critical aspects of any business. There is no better way than the quality way, because that means we make a quality product at the fastest rate possible for a minimal cost.

Once we have decided what our value proposition to a customer will be, total quality management will guarantee that you will be making it available in the most effective and efficient way. The idea that quality and productivity are conflicting characteristics has been with us for way too long.

It is a false contradiction as this has first been proven by the Japanese, and later on by companies all over the world. We have learned that quality methods are not just useful to improve the quality of a product, but even more so, to improve the overall results of an organisation. Making the same product quicker, and at lower cost, makes the process of higher quality just like reducing quality errors at the same speed for the same cost is an increase in the quality of the process.

By eliminating waste, avoiding a bad product, using less energy and raw materials, as well as many other elements of improved processes, we do contribute to the prime objective of reducing the overall costs and increasing profit margins.

In doing so, there is another effect of quality management emerging: we contribute to the environmental sustainability of our organisations.

Even within the quality world, this is not always recognised as such.

Integrating quality, environmental care and safety into one overall management system is a very positive evolution. It creates awareness for the links between these important aspects for any organisation.

However, the contribution of quality methods and tools to the environmental sustainability of any organisation should be much more emphasised. Throughout its history, quality management has developed an extensive body of knowledge on improvement projects. This is equally applicable to improving the environmental impact of a company as it is to improve the quality of the products produced. These improvement projects show that sustainability and competitiveness go hand-in-hand and are not opposites, as so often is stated.

Obviously, these are small and local contributions, and in the grand scheme of environmental things, they may look like small positive drops in an ocean of negativity. However, this judgement on the impact that quality management has on environmental sustainability is rather harsh.

Even the most torrential rain consists of individual drops, so to have a bigger impact, you just need to generate more drops.

If more organisations understand the power of quality management tools, and actively use them to enhance their economic, social and environmental sustainability, this will improve. Multiplying the application with more projects in organisations will have a noticeable impact.

In addition, quality can directly impact that grand environmental scheme of things: the overall system. However, this is a much harder challenge to tackle. It does not only require quality knowledge, but also quite a lot of courage and perseverance.

What really is the goal of environmental sustainability? Definitely not *'To Save The Planet.'* The planet has been here long before us and will be here long after us. It has proven to be perfectly capable of taking care of itself. Thinking it needs saving by us is a typical example of the ridiculous arrogance of Homo Sapiens.

Unfortunately, this arrogance can also be found in the most important known definition of sustainable development that was defined by the 1987 United Nations (UN) Brundtland Commission:

> ***Sustainable development is development that meets the needs of the present generation without compromising the ability of future generations to meet their own needs.***

Although over thirty-five years old, this is still the reference definition, often cited and treated with great respect.

The definition, however, contains two weak points. The first flaw is that it talks about present and future generations of only one species: ours! Of course the report contained a lot of annexes, and has ultimately led to the 17

Sustainable Development Goals (SDG's) of the United Nations that claim to offer a balanced scorecard. Nevertheless, within this definition, you could refer to a development as being sustainable, so long as people thrive, even at the expense of other species. The current mass extinction of species in this Anthropocentric era may be a consequence of our single species thinking.

The second flaw is that no limits are set to the needs that must be met for present and future generations. This is fully in line with our economic system of infinite growth.

During my first year of engineering studies, we had a course on basic economics. The course tutor was Baron André Vlerick, a former finance minister in the Belgian government. In one of his first lessons, he explained that the goal of a country's economy had to be to satisfy the needs of its population; a statement which is very much in line with the sustainable development definition cited above.

"However," he added, "I do not agree with my American colleague who says that we have to make them want that pink refrigerator."

He did not agree with the creation of new and artificial needs, but of course, this is in total contradiction to the growth economy he propagated. Growth is a very simple system: more people continuously need to buy more stuff. Like a pink refrigerator that in Barbie movie times must undoubtedly be very popular. A tip for marketeers.

Because, to keep this going, you need marketing. No profession has grown as much as the marketing profession. Sometimes, I think there are more people making their money with convincing others to buy products they do not need, than there are people actually producing these products.

Within this context, it was interesting to observe the consumption patterns during the first stages of the Covid 19 crisis. Needs were brought back to their bare essentials: toilet paper and pasta. We watched as the whole economic system crumbled to pieces and governments all over the world were desperately looking for ways *to get people consuming again*.

Many books have tried to define the meaning of life, but in our developed society, it is extremely simple: you are a human resource, and the meaning of your life is to produce and consume as much as possible.

Our definition of progress, not contradicted by the one for classical sustainable development, has been, and still is: *more*. As a counter-movement, many environmentalists today state that to save the ecosystems, we have to go for less; using a more modern term: *degrow*. A controversial statement and not very appealing to the poor of today.

There is also some Western arrogance in this. We do not want Brazilians to cut the rain forest, but we easily forget that we have destroyed as good as all the major forests in Europe for our own economic development. It is as if South Americans ought to be punished for being too late to destroy their rain forests.

Of course, both views are fundamentally wrong. There is only one word that expresses true progress: *better*. An improvement in the quality of life is the only way by which we may express progress; not just human life, but the quality of all life. In some places, for certain elements, that will be more; in other places and/or for other elements, it will be less.

Many places are in need of more food, sanitation facilities, and easy access to water that is drinkable. In our developed world however, most problems are related to having *too much*: obesity because of *too much* food, traffic jams from *too many* cars, and global warming because of *too much* use of energy.

We could be a lot healthier with less, but better food or drink. One could, for instance, stop drinking six packs of Bud Light and replace them by one glass of beer. Real beer, I mean. Why not try a Belgian beer and replace the quantity of consumption by the quality of consumption, and enjoy more?

Development can only be defined as truly sustainable, if the end result is better for the entire ecosystem, humans included. Hence, my proposal for a new definition:

> *"Sustainable development means that the present generation takes the necessary actions to pass on our unique biosphere to the next generation in a better state than it was received. And so on..."*

To summarise: '*All Life Matters.*'

There are many reasons to work on the biosphere improvement, and the most mentioned being to safeguard our species, as we are just a part of that ecosystem. We do not need to save the planet; it is ourselves that we need to save. The fast reduction of biodiversity is a serious problem; according to many biologists it is even more urgent and critical than global warming. One typical example is the loss of flying insects, which is seen as a threat to the food chain, and as such, a direct threat to us.

People are ingenious; so, maybe we can develop technology to such a level that we do not need that ecosystem to support us. Maybe we can live in a society with only species of use to us, and without any wild nature. But do we want to live in such a world?

After a trip to Alaska, I mentioned to the quality manager at a customer's site that we had seen grizzly bears, and how impressive these animals were. Well, they were to us, but clearly not to him. He saw bears of any colour as big, wild and dangerous animals, with no use whatsoever.

His exact response was:
"Why do bears have to exist?"

Believe me, it is not easy to explain why bears must exist. In all honesty: I think it is impossible to prove that bears – or any other species, including our own – need to exist.

On the World Wildlife Fund (WWF) website, there is a list of endangered animals. At the top, you find the critically endangered species like the Amur Leopard, the Bornean Orangutan, the Sunda Tiger, the Lowland Gorilla and so on. Reading this list, you realise there is only one good reason why all these species need to exist as part of our ecosystem: their radiant beauty.

A poor farmer in Namibia plants red flowers in his garden to make his life better by enjoying its beauty. We are rich, but for exactly the same reason we need to restore and preserve the biosphere. Guaranteeing that all that beauty will still be out there and thriving, makes our lives and that of future generations better. We simply cannot afford to lose all that beauty!

COLUMN 2
PERFECTIONISM KILLS

Le mieux est l'ennemi du bien
A French proverb

Reality television is extremely popular, but tends to be rather vulgar; this perhaps explains why it is so popular. However, every now and then, there is an interesting series that I get attracted to, so I would like to draw your attention to *"Top Doctors"* on Belgian Television.

It has been running for several years, and has remained relevant and fascinating. It follows doctors, generally surgeons, that perform some highly advanced and critical operations, in their professional and personal lives, but in a non-intrusive and respectful way.

The only thing that bothers me is its title, or rather the *"Top"* part of the title. When you read an article about a lawsuit, the lawyers involved are inevitably top lawyers. Only top players are active in football and top writers in literature, and of course, there are only top politicians. The latter should already make us a bit suspicious about the value of all these so-called *top* people. It fits into a general trend of a dislike of the average, the normal, the regular.

On LinkedIn, a lot of people identify with the following slogan: '*I am not here to be average, I am here to be awesome.*' It sounds impressive, but people using this statement make three mistakes: they do not understand the meaning of average, they cannot define awesome, and they almost certainly overrate themselves. The latter is actually what most people tend to do.

I was in a session once where the speaker performed an experiment with the audience. He asked us to position ourselves in contrast with our professional peers. Then he asked us to shut our eyes, and that those who considered themselves to belong in the top 5% of their profession, raise their hands and keep them raised. Gradually, he went up to top 10%, top 20%, top 30%, top 50% and then he told everyone to open their eyes. Lo and behold, all hands were raised. So, all the people in that audience claimed to belong to the top 50% of their profession.

In their own eyes, they were all above average; by definition, a mathematical impossibility.

A friend of mine recently told me a similar story. In a session with medical doctors, the speaker said, with some level of authority, that half of them had to be below average. This led to a very fierce discussion with the audience claiming this could not be true.

Amazing, really! With at least seven years of university studies, they still had not grasped what average meant. Most people will be at, or about the average, and there is nothing wrong with that, even if we find it hard to accept.

It is sometimes claimed that only chronically depressed people have a correct view of where they stand in life. This is not a very uplifting thought, so maybe we need this overestimation to be able to function.

Of course, some people do excel, but no one outshines everyone else at everything. When people say they are here to be awesome, one could ask what it is exactly they want to be awesome in. They may want to be an awesome manager, an awesome colleague, an awesome parent, an awesome friend or maybe an awesome lover.

Probably they would want to be 'an awesome everything.' I am afraid that will prove to be too massive an ambition. But it expresses the desire to be special, which of course, we all are, and not because we are awesome in everything, but because we are all unique in all sorts of ways. Special, just like everybody else.

In some things, we are probably uniquely bad and there is nothing wrong with that either.

Now let us return to the top doctors. It was one of them who referred to the French proverb in the subtitle: "*Le mieux est l'ennemi du bien.*" This translates into "*The best is the enemy of good.*" To him, it was a key aspect of quality in surgery; to me, it was something of a shock.

I had never heard it before, and it goes against everything I had been taught in quality. If I were to present this to an audience of quality professionals, then I would have to announce it with '...*pardon my French.*'

In the meantime, I have learned that there is also an English equivalent, but it sounds much nicer in French. I do not think anyone doubts the importance of quality in surgery, so how can it be that the best is worse than good, and could this also be valid outside of surgery?

Imagine you are a surgeon and your operation is almost finished. You have connected the veins back to the organ, blood starts flowing, the organ starts working, there are no leaks and all patient parameters are normal, but you observe one of the stitches is not perfectly placed. Then the message is: *leave it, it is good enough*! Do not remove that stitch and try to replace it with a better placed one because, 'L*e mieux est l'ennemi du bien.*' It is better for the patient if you leave this alone. What is important to note here is that each patient is different.

The definition of perfect does not really exist, but you can judge – as a surgeon – if the result is good enough. This does not mean there is no search for improvement. The doctors who participate in the television programme referred to above, are often world authorities in their field because they have developed new ways of operating for a certain deficiency. There is a higher level of continual improvement going on, but even in this new improved method in each operation, it is important to know when to stop, when it is good enough.

Good enough is also a term that has been used for parenting as a reaction to all the books trying to turn you into the perfect (*awesome?*) parent, a goal no one will ever achieve. Again, there is no overall definition of perfect. Each parent is different, every child is different, and both vary in time. In a nutshell, what works for one child might not work for another, even in the same household. And what works today might not work tomorrow. We all have good and bad days, and our patience with a child's behaviour can be dramatically different from one moment to the other.

In quality, we often use the term excellence, and you find this in different combinations like operational excellence, business excellence, and also in quality for excellence, where quality is seen as a means to reach the illusive excellence target.

Seeing excellence or perfection as a target is where things go wrong.

The problem is that it is an indefinable and shifting target; what is excellent today can, by tomorrow, be unacceptable, or completely outdated. The only thing you can say is that it is a never-ending journey on a wobbly road driven by continual improvement. This is by all means a positive endeavour, but we have a tendency to focus on the negatives of that endeavour.

In quality management, we actually rarely talk about quality. We are mainly concerned about, and busy with non-quality: customer complaints, cost of rejects, corrective actions, etc. To such an extent that when people see a quality professional approaching their work place, they are already wondering what went wrong this time. We rarely congratulate and thank people for the quality level we have already reached, or for the amazing things we are capable of doing, and that we do day in, and day out.

> ***We all have procedures on how to handle customer complaints, but very few, if any, have a procedure on how to handle customer compliments.***

This is equally important feedback.

I have listened to many end-of-year speeches by CEOs and plant managers, and they all go like this: '*We have done really well this year, but...*' And the whole thing is immediately ruined because there follows a whole list of things that need to be better. We all know that, and there is no need to repeat it; try to be positive and grateful for what people have achieved in the past year.

Striving for excellence means telling people to run a marathon with the added difficulty that the finish line, which at the start is 42.195 kilometres away, will be moved farther during the race. No athlete would even start under such conditions. However, this is what is asked of your people in the strive for excellence. If the only thing you are offering them to keep going is the shifting target distance, they will all give up. And some will collapse.

Perfectionism has been linked with serious psychological problems like performance anxiety and suicide; hence, the title of this Column, *Perfectionism Kills*. Every now and then we have to stand still and celebrate what we have achieved. Given the fiercely competitive environment we live in, all organisations have achieved amazing things so far; otherwise, they would no longer exist.

> *The real issue is to find joy in improvement: enjoying the running itself, rather than only focusing on reaching the finish line.*

The former chief editor of the Belgian weekly magazine, HUMO, was Guy Mortier. He had no problem declaring himself a perfectionist, and he did not even understand how this could be a problem. His ambition was very simple and constant: *'This week I want us to make the best HUMO we ever made.'*

Clearly, this is impossible to achieve week after week. Something he realised and accepted, but not without trying each week. It takes a strong personality to keep trying, despite knowing you will often fail. Only if the organisation has fun in trying and can accept failure, can you keep this up.

Modern quality management has been developed in industry, in mass production environments where there is a drawing with specifications and the task is to try and make all products equal to the nominal value on that drawing for all characteristics. In other words: eliminate variation and standardise. Much of this is valid in large areas of the industry, and the tools developed to achieve this are a big help. However, technological advancements and changes in customer expectations do inflict a serious impact and require different thinking about quality.

Some twenty years ago, I did some consultancy work on implementing a quality management system, in conformance to ISO 9001, within a small company that delivered IT components to industry. As one of the first steps of the project, I carried out an awareness session with the management team.

I gave some explanation about the Standard and how to apply this within their business. One of the participants did not like the word, *standard*, not just ISO 9001, but standard in general. He had a new kitchen being installed at home, and when talking to potential suppliers, they constantly used the word, standard, too: height of the tables, height of the sink, depth of closets, etc.

Each time, he made the same remark to the salesperson: "I am not standard."

He actually was not, he was close to two meters tall!

Most office chairs are very adaptable and have been like that for many years. You can adjust the height and tilt the back support to such an extent that you can comfortably put your feet on your desk and have a little powernap. Strangely, all this flexibility happened in front of a fixed and massive desk.

Only recently, desks have been made more flexible, and now you can even switch to working standing up. This also gives you the option to find a combined position of chair and desk allowing you to nap even more comfortably. In any event, flexibility and adaptability are important requirements.

Customers are not there to adapt to your standards: you are there to adapt to their needs.

This is a lesson to remember to pass on to your design department, because this pressure for much more personalised solutions to customer needs, is one of the most important trends in industry. As a result, we are required to produce a bigger variety of products in smaller series, but making sure that all parts are within specification. This is a serious challenge.

A highly flexible production infrastructure with similar accuracy and speed is required. Fortunately, we have help from technological improvements, often summarised as *Industry 4.0*: this includes automation, artificial intelligence, internet of things, big data, 3D printing, machine learning, and the like.

We are getting closer to how Warren Bennis sees the factory of the future; an organisation that will have only two employees: a man and a dog. The man is there to feed the dog, the dog is there to keep the man from touching the machines. We are not there yet, and perhaps will never get there. The possibilities of technologies are often overestimated and the flexibility of people underestimated, but this is the direction we are going. We are keeping our ideal of product perfection but adapting to individual customer requirements through a different process of manufacturing.

Digitisation also offers another solution to this problem: standardise hardware and take care of the individual requirements through software. This change requires a completely different mindset because if you stick to your belief in perfection, there will be serious negative impacts. In our fast-changing digitised world, these negative impacts could even become a threat to the survival of your organisation. It needs a drastic rethinking of your product design process to overcome that threat.

The design process has several stages, but in the end, the objective is to turn an idea into a product design that can fulfil all customer needs and be produced profitably. Once the design is finished, at least 80% of everything related to the product is defined: these include cost, customer satisfaction, manufacturability, serviceability, recyclability... Many cost-saving projects are happening in production, but they only work on the remaining 20% of the total cost; surely, this is not a very effective approach.

At some point in time, the company I worked for was confronted with the following dilemma: design a new product or produce the existing product at a lower cost. To evaluate the possibilities of the latter, everyone was asked to come up with ideas for cost reductions. There were lots of ideas, but management was not happy with them. Most ideas required engineering changes, and that was not the objective of the exercise. Management was looking for ideas on how to produce the same product more efficiently, but the possibilities of that proved to be very limited. In short: it is the design, stupid!

In a software-dominated environment, some absolute truths about the design process are being challenged. It is like a key rule that I learned early on about design:

The shortest way to bankruptcy are engineering changes.

When you look at quality systems and tools that have been developed to control the design process, you will see that a lot of them are aimed at reducing the risk of engineering changes. There is also the added consideration that the later in the process a change is made, the more costly it becomes.

Correcting a dimension on a drawing is easy and cheap but once the design has been released and the product has been produced and delivered, correcting a design error becomes terribly expensive. So, it is logical and good that quality professionals want to make sure that the design is complete, and error- and risk-free before it is released. This is one reason why they are not always liked by the design engineers, because they tend to slow down the process. However, everybody realises how costly changes can be, so reviews, controls and testing are accepted.

Today, the performance of an increasing variety of products is defined by software, and no longer by hardware. *Big Data* analysis allows us to understand the satisfaction or dissatisfaction of customers with the product in an extremely detailed and fast way.

Artificial Intelligence programmes can analyse the experiences of users and turn them into software updates, as a basis to improve performance.

With the *Internet of Things*, there is a permanent connectivity with all products, so changing the software becomes a matter of launching the update, and within seconds all products worldwide have had performance improved, increased functionality, or whatever it is the change was proposed to deliver.

If we stick to perfectionism in this new world, what happens? We only want to release a product if we are sure there are no risks left and all functionality has been foreseen and tested. But the possibilities of software are inexhaustible. We will never be able to implement 'all' functionality. In addition, the people defining perfection are the design engineers and the quality engineers. We, as producers, will define what perfection is and when it has been reached. But with all due respect: that is irrelevant. The only real judge of your product will be the customer.

Aiming for perfection prior to release in a software-driven world, will be like waiting for Godot in Samuel Beckett's play: endless.

It is much smarter to opt to increasingly add functionalities, rather than wait with the release until it is perfect. You will be hopelessly late on the market to discover that your customers have another idea about perfection, and you will be forced to change the software anyway. So, in current designs with high software impact, perfectionism actually can kill your product before it is even released.

In a digitised age, we need more agility and concepts like *Minimal Viable Product*, become key in the development process. Release a product that has basic functionality, offers a service to customers and has gone through a risk analysis. Gather information from your customers as they use it, and improve the product based on their feedback.

Sometimes, cars have been described as smartphones on wheels, because of their dependence on software. But even very simple products are software driven today. A good example is smart lighting systems. They are extremely simple to install and offer a lot of personalisation possibilities through a wide range of functionality that is regularly updated. And this is another thing that has changed: customers are no longer annoyed by software changes, they are used to it, and they are actually expecting it.

Even a boomer like me has gotten acquainted with it. I am notified of changes in my MS Office 365 package, but never read the accompanying mail (I would not understand it anyway), and I see what has changed. Sometimes it is interesting and I start using it; other times, I do not pay attention because it does not affect me. Some years ago, though, I absolutely hated software changes.

Another important aspect to do with striving for excellence is problem-solving; this is one of the things quality is very good at. A lot of the various methods we have developed are aimed at exactly that: solving problems. This goes from the Plan-Do-Check-Act approaches to more complex ones, but fundamentally similar methods, like Six Sigma. We create a stepwise project framework, add a set of appropriate tools to each step, and by disciplined application of the method and the tools, we come to a solution to the problem.

All these methodologies are extremely powerful. It would benefit many organisations to apply them more and better. Ideally, you can find the so-called root cause(s) of the problem, and once this is known, we can come up with a suitable solution. Problem-solving approaches and root cause analysis are very effective when dealing with technical problems where data gathering and analysis are possible. Do note though that not all problems are technical.

We praise ourselves for our creativity and problem-solving power. It has undeniably led us to an increase in quality of life, among other things seen in the quantity of life. We live longer and in better health. There is no doubt that we have improved, though we are continuously confronted with new challenges. To me, this is because we overestimate the effectiveness and applicability of our problem-solving capabilities when we are dealing with complex problems.

In essence, we never solve problems. We replace them by new ones that are less serious, or at least, that we hope will be less serious.

Sustainable Development Goal (SDG) 2 of the United Nations' 17 SDGs, aims at "Zero Hunger," a noble aspiration, for sure. The percentage of the world population suffering from food shortages has been drastically reduced over the last 200 years.

Currently, the value is about 10%, and represents some 800 million people; all in all, still shameful in our rich world. But that is not the point I want to make here. Along with this remarkable improvement, another statistic shows a totally different trend.

Since 1975, worldwide obesity has nearly tripled. In fact, in many parts of the world today, overweight and obesity kill more people than undernourishment.

Our remarkable improvement has replaced the problem of not enough food with the new problem of too much food. Soon the number of obese people on the planet will be higher than the number of undernourished people. This has significant health consequences.

Hunger must be a horrible thing, and it is something that very few of us have ever experienced.

The stress of waking up in the morning not knowing if you will find enough food to feed your children during the day must be close to unbearable.

So, probably the new obesity problem is not as severe as the hunger problem that it has replaced, but it cannot be ignored either.

The massive use of fossil fuels has contributed enormously to the development of our society: an industrial revolution, mass access to electricity and heating, movement of goods and people, creating an explosion of trade and a phenomenal growth in tourism, the development of new products like plastics; the list is endless. However, it has also created new problems like the plastic soup in our oceans, and the global warming of our planet. These new problems have similar characteristics: they become apparent very slowly, often only long after the introduction of instantly beneficial changes, and they pose a global threat. Perhaps the created new problems will prove to be bigger than the solved ones.

Perfectionism can play a negative part in the problem-solving process itself. Traffic jams are one of the biggest problems in Belgium, especially around the cities of Antwerp and Brussels. For this major problem, the root cause is surprisingly simple: too many cars at the same time in the same place.

Because of the increasingly negative impact of traffic jams on the economy, different institutions have come up with possible solutions. With every new proposal, the involved specialist is interviewed on television, and each time the same question is asked: "*Will this be **the** solution to the traffic jam problem?*"

It is often said that there are no stupid questions, but anyone who watches television regularly knows there are loads of stupid questions and this one is a perfect – no pun intended – example.

Of course, this is not **the** solution to the problem. If it were that simple, we would never have had traffic jams in the first place. But maybe it can alleviate the situation a little, reduce the length and/or the number of traffic jams. That improvement gives us extra room to think about additional actions to improve the situation further.

> *If we want to solve a problem with one action leading to immediate perfection, we often end up doing nothing.*

Never forget that action is the only thing that leads to change. You can analyse a problem to death, but without action, it will not go away. Reducing the nuisance problem by 10% is better than endlessly waiting for the perfect solution. Remember, Godot has still not arrived!

COLUMN 3
ALL ERRORS ARE
HUMAN ERRORS

*A bad system will beat a good person
every time*
Dr W E Deming

The title and subtitle of this Column may seem a little contradictory to you, and you are right, they are, and deliberately so. The title is mine, but the subtitle is a quote from one of the best known and most admired quality gurus.

Now, gurus come in all shapes and sizes, but quality gurus have a couple of very similar characteristics. They are all men, all passed away, they are American or Japanese, and they all did their most important work forty to sixty years ago. And today, if you ask the internet for a top thirty list of most influential management gurus, none of them are on it.

Personally, I think this observation should get us worried about the importance and influence quality has in today's business. This, though, is not applicable to the quality community at large, as quotes of our gurus are filling up social media, and are endlessly repeated. It goes as far as some competition about who is the most important quality guru and how big his contribution and legacy were. This may seem futile to you, dear reader, but make no mistake, this is serious business among quality professionals. I am always amazed, and I have to admit also slightly amused, when discussions like that are being held on LinkedIn.

You would be surprised how fierce some of these discussions become. This is a logical consequence of being a guru follower: there is a risk of a slight (or heavy) loss of critical thinking, and a tendency to almost deify a person. Comments on the work are seen as comments on the person, and you may be accused of blasphemy.

As indicated, some people are currently much more admired than quality gurus, and Elon Musk is high on that list. He is also active on social media, even owning one right now, and he has loads of followers. On a recent (and recurring) post, there was a referral to the following so-called Elon Musk quote: "*I hate when people confuse education with intelligence. You can have a bachelor's degree and still be an idiot.*"

This post had a lot of success, and that puzzled me for two reasons. First of all, many people agreed with the statement and reacted as if Musk had actually invented it. That someone without a degree can be more intelligent than someone with a degree, has been said by millions all over the world from the very moment degrees existed, generally by people who do not have a degree.

The biggest problem however, lies in the quote itself. The way it is stated it is impossible to argue against.

It states a possibility without a probability and consequently, it is both undeniably true and totally meaningless.

Yes, some people can have a degree and be idiots, just like people without a degree can be intelligent, but does that say anything about the value of a degree, or formal education? You can smoke a pack of cigarettes a day and live to be 100 years old, but does that tell us anything about the impact of smoking on a person's life expectancy? You can live a sex and drugs and rock 'n roll life, and at 80 years, still be on stage, have a 34-year-old girlfriend and a 7-year-old kid, but how many of us do compare to Mick Jagger? However, yes you can! Maybe.

In one of my more stupid moments, I reacted to the post, claiming that messages like this cast doubt on the value of education in a world where there are millions of children (mainly girls) who have no access to formal education at all. Their lives could be improved drastically if they had the opportunity to attend school, learn new things, and possibly pursue a degree. A young engineer and Musk enthusiast found it necessary to put me right and he used a special sentence to make things clear to me: *"You do not get it!"*

In the Introduction to this book, I indicated that the inspiration for the title came from Julian Barnes. The above sentence plays a key role in one of the best novels ever written by him (and anyone else for that matter): *The Sense of an Ending*. For a moment, I felt like Tony Webster, the main character in the book, who was getting exactly the same reply several times over, and when he eventually got it, he understood the drama that had hit an old and special friend. I will say no more, just do what engineers are so often told to do: RTFB (Read The F**king Book)!

I explained why the statement was useless, and that for once, I did get it, but never got a reply.

Admiration can get worse though. After a SpaceX rocket had exploded during a test flight, there were a lot of comments on Twitter, both negative (as always, it is Twitter, even if it is renamed as X[1]) and positive, indicating that the company had learned from its failure. This is quite in line with my thinking in this book. However, it was all ruined when one of the admirers felt it necessary to praise the sustainability of the SpaceX programme.

Triumphantly, he tweeted: *"Elon does not use fossil fuel for his rockets, he uses methane!"*

So many people have made major contributions to the universal development of quality management. These men have been important, and we all stand on their gigantic shoulders.

> ***I just wished we did not call them gurus, and kept a critical view on their work, and in particular, on the value of it in today's business environment.***

Very few truths are eternal, and the world has changed. Let us take as an example, in an environment where customers are looking for personalised experiences, standardising and

---

[1] Elon Musk, who purchased Twitter, changed the name to X in April 2023.

removing variation might not be the best approach to satisfy them.

When I state that all errors are human errors, it is often heavily contested within the quality community, specifically referring to the Deming quote above. The problem, they say, is not the human error but the bad system. There is even a tendency to turn this quote into saying that if the system were good, all work within that system would automatically be good, so somehow, the system is always to blame. There is a simple linguistic reason for this: when the term, *human error* is used in quality, and even in society at large, what people actually mean is *operator error*.

> ***For some reason, there is a firm belief that managers – the ones developing the systems – are not really part of humanity.***

They are seen as somewhat humanoid creatures (from a distance), aiming and forcing workers into mistakes by generating toxic systems for them to work and fail in. Little Darth Vaders creating bad systems in their small evil empires.

A statement often used concerning operator error is: '*No one enters the factory with the intention of doing a bad job, or causing harm.*' I fully agree with that, so why would managers enter their offices with the intention to create bad systems? All these humans work together trying to create the best possible outcome for the organisation, and they all make mistakes. The rare ones that do not, probably, are those that do not do much at all. These so-called 'bad systems' were designed, developed and implemented by humans with the best of intentions. And just like an operator does not intentionally make mistakes, the system builders do not get pleasure out of building bad systems.

On Friday September 22, 2006, an experimental magnetic levitation (maglev) train collided during a test run with a maintenance vehicle near Lathen in Germany. The tragic crash resulted in twenty-three people being killed. Immediately, the question was raised as to whether it was a human error or a technical error.

You can see how deeply this wrong thinking pattern and use of words is embedded in society. With *human error*, an error by the train driver or the people responsible for the vehicle maintenance on the track was meant. The investigation showed that indeed a chain of errors made by these people led to the collision and some were convicted for it.

Suppose it turned out that what was referred to as a *technical error* was the cause of the accident. Would the conclusion then be that no human being was responsible? That seems highly unlikely to me. Maglev trains simply do not grow on trees; we have invented them, by turning an idea into a product to enable the movement of more people faster and with better efficiency from point A to B.

Just like anything in our society is an idea from people turned into a product or service by people. Further investigation would have ended up with some mistake made by someone somewhere in the process: bad design, faulty material, wrong welding, unclear instructions, and so on. All these potential causes have one thing in common: there are always humans behind them.

Nature does not make mistakes, although it can be very ruthless and knows little to zero mercy. It evolves at random, with no objective and no meaning, but to perpetuate its own existence. We, on the other hand, can purposely create things. Whatever goes wrong with what we have created is, by definition, related to human error.

People are always responsible for their actions, no matter if they are managers or operators. However, that does not mean they are guilty and should be prosecuted for their mistakes. Words matter! If we could get rid of our blame culture, we could take a major step forward within our organisations and our communities. Regrettably, we live in a highly legalised society. There is this obsession that someone must be found guilty for whatever goes wrong. Contrary to what is thought, once the guilty party is found and convicted, the problem is not necessarily solved, most often it is not.

> *Our tolerance for an honest mistake is at an all-time low and social media does not help, to make an understatement.*

Statements like the one from Dr Deming do not help either. Even if it is not meant as such, it leads to some sort of divide between the people working within the same organisation. Of course, there are questionable managers and bad systems, but operators will also make mistakes.

Putting all the blame on management and systems is too easy, even given that they do bear the higher responsibility as their authority and decisions have a bigger impact. What is actually needed to grow as an organisation is more cooperation, closer contact between organisational layers as well as a much better understanding of the inherent complexity and difficulties that any job is confronted with, operational or managerial.

Claiming operator errors are, to a large extent, due to the system not only reduces the responsibility, but also the importance and impact of operators on the quality of product or service. If operator errors have little to do with the operator, it does not matter who the operator is.

In the early days of ISO 9001 certifications, a marketing manager of a freshly certified Irish food chain in an interview said: "*Thanks to our certified quality management system, we can now replace any worker, and that will not affect our quality.*" If that were the case, and I was the CEO, I would immediately replace my expensive marketing manager with the first unemployed guy passing by.

My father was, what is called today, an unskilled labourer. A ridiculous term because he possessed loads of skills. He used to work in the glass industry, and in construction, to name but a few. To him, there was a good way of doing things and a bad way too, and he took pride in doing things in the best possible way. Believe me, operators themselves know there are good and not-so-good operators; in their judgement, they tend to be much clearer and harder than their managers.

> ***Besides, how could anyone take pride out of a job that whether or not it was done well, has nothing to do with them?***

A job cannot exempt people from the responsibility for the quality of that job. In all systems, good or bad, you will see people doing good work, and occasionally bad work.

Fortunately, I think that the situation today has changed for the better from what pertained to Dr Deming's time. Operators are no longer the victims of a system, but they increasingly contribute to the design of the system. They are more outspoken, and will point out weaknesses. In this way, they contribute to the quality of the products and services in the organisation, not only by doing a good job, but also by helping to improve the system. They use their brains and take responsibility, also for their errors. If you do not want that, replace them with robots and see where it gets you.

The above, however, does not mean systems are not important and do not require changing and improving, quite the opposite. An additional challenge with systems is that they can be extremely firm, and often very hard to alter because some are deeply embedded in our society and our thinking patterns. They are said to suffer from *TINA* thinking "*There Is No Alternative.*" There is, of course, always an alternative, and more so, even many different possibilities. They may not necessarily be better, but they do exist.

For some years, I did a lot of consulting work with a car manufacturer on several aspects of quality and maintenance. The coffee machine at their engineering department was close to a large window, which gave a view of the road in front of the factory. This road is the main traffic axis through the industrial harbour area where the car manufacturer is located. I recall one day having coffee with one of the engineers and we were watching a major traffic jam in front of us.

"It is like that every day with every shift change," the engineer said. "We have these huge traffic jams several times a day, and year by year it just gets worse and worse," he continued. His obvious conclusion was:

There are simply too many cars on the road.

I just nodded in agreement but could not help thinking that here we were in a factory where all employees, my coffee companion included, were working very hard in the hope that they could sell more cars of their brand. It was clear that they were directly responsible for, and adding to, the problem that stood before us. Actually, I, helping them to do that better and more efficiently, was also adding to the problem. It shows how strong systems can be.

Now cars are special things that are filled with emotion. I think that is the main reason why they still exist as individual means of transport. Elon Musk, here he is again, has convinced the world that replacing fossil fuel cars with electric cars will save the environment. Tesla is now worth more than as good as its competitors put together.

I do not think this says anything about Tesla or its competitors, it is more a sign of the complete ridiculousness of modern economics. To avoid getting into this dangerous discussion field (I already took a huge risk by doubting a statement by Dr Deming), and being an engineer myself, I will focus on the technical aspects.

A Tesla is a big metal box, carrying its own engine and source of energy, weighing about two tons and generally used to transport one 80-kilogramme person, most often from home to work and back.

Basically, it is hardly different from the cars that were made one hundred years ago. To be correct, I must add that most of the time a car is doing absolutely nothing at all. It stands in the office car park for eight hours, and a little later in front of your house for another twelve to fourteen hours.

I am pretty confident that the average coffee machine in a typical office has a much higher overall equipment efficiency (*OEE*, for the specialists) than the car you drive. If you had a machine in your factory with that kind of efficiency, you would outsource the process immediately.

It is only those that are stuck in a system that would think privately owned cars are the solution to people's movement, that can say electric cars are the future. Traffic jams are not shorter when filled with electric vehicles, and as already shown, they are equally inefficient as any other car. In cities, you could better replace fossil fuel cars with electric bikes: it is cheaper, has lower energy consumption and it is much healthier for you and the citizens.

The future of transport should follow the software industry: transport on demand and movement as a service. High-speed trains for inter-city transport are a highly effective public transportation system, and maybe a car (or even better, a bike) on demand for the last mile. All of this will depend on the willingness of people to trade the romantic feeling of owning their car for the logic of a functional system.

Do not underestimate the feeling of power of mastering this two-tonne metal box or the joy of driving. We wrongly think people are rational beings functioning on pure logic. Apart from technical and legal problems, the feeling of being in control when driving might be a bigger obstacle to self-driving cars than was ever imagined.

What about some really big systems like the economy and the planetary climate system? Links are being made between the two, specifically about the potential effect of global warming on the economy.

Many institutions have commented on this; the United Nations, the Organisation for Economic Co-operation and Development (OECD), the International Monetary Fund

(IMF), the World Bank and so on. The various statements are rather similar and sound something like this: '*Global warming may cost up to Y% of the economy by 20xx.*' This seems to indicate that global warming is causing economic problems. Putting it differently: '*You naughty planet, heating up and threatening our beautiful economy,*' is clearly a cause-effect relationship.

In quality, we learn to look for the root cause. The main cause concerning global warming is the exhaust of greenhouse gasses (GHG), with CO_2 being the biggest and best known. Elon Musk's methane (CH_4) is also on that list. One way to avoid global warming causing problems for the economy is of course to reduce GHG emissions in general, and CO_2 emissions in particular.

The first thing to do is to see how CO_2 emissions are evolving; we are data-driven professionals after all. With a bit of luck, they are already dropping, and we do not need to do anything. Is optimism not a moral duty?

Sadly, in this case, it is not realistic because over the last twenty-five years, worldwide CO_2 emissions have been rising year by year. With two noticeable exceptions: 2009 and 2020. It is interesting to study outliers and specifically to see if they have anything in common. We are lucky, they do: both years saw a deep and global economic crisis. In 2009, it was the consequence of the financial crisis, and in 2020, it was caused by the Covid-19 pandemic.

I hear a lot of proposals to reduce CO2 emissions, often based on not yet existing or scalable technology. That is all great and needs to be developed further; however, over the last twenty-five years technological development was not forbidden, but it clearly was not able to bend the curve downwards.

> ***So far, the only thing that has proven to work to reduce GHG exhausts on a global scale, is a global economic crisis.***

Could it not be that the cause-effect relationship is actually the other way around? Is it not the case that our economic system fuels global warming, which subsequently causes problems for the economy? Perhaps our economic system bites its own tail!

Just a thought, but I would think, given the data, it is worthy of further investigation. After all, if something is wrong with a man-made system it can be corrected by man-made actions. We do not need to continuously make the same human error.

COLUMN 4
"WHAT A LOAD OF RUBBISH"

English Football Chant

My parents had six children, but there was an age gap of twenty-five years between me, the youngest, and Laura, my oldest sister. When I was born in 1955, she had a four-year-old toddler and was pregnant with her second child. I was literally a born uncle. As a consequence, despite being born into a large family, I only lived in a large family for a short time. By the time I finished high school, it was only my parents and I who still lived in our house.

Shortly after my high school years, in my first semester at university, my mother committed suicide. I have always found this to be a strange combination of words, as it contains an element of action, and consequently, guilt, to be compared with someone who committed murder. On the contrary, she was a victim of her thoughts, fears and anxieties. As it stands today, I am the only one of all the family members who is left.

This is logical when one is the youngest, but a strange feeling, nevertheless.

Anyway, it was just my dad and I that lived in our family house during my engineering course studies. I commuted from Bruges to Ghent, so I was at home every evening. That period was also the start of *Cable Television*, and in the area where we lived, close to the Belgian coast, we had access to the British channels BBC1, BBC2 and ITV. Being able to watch these channels greatly helped improve my English language skills. I advise everyone to let their children watch foreign television channels where they use subtitles instead of versions dubbed by ridiculous voices.

I played soccer back then, and had (and still have) a big love for the game. I always watched "*Match of the Day*" when the late Jimmy Hill ran the show. It was rather late when the programme started, so my father was usually in bed while I, on my own, enjoyed the Premier League football updates, which at the time was called *The Football League First Division*.

Liverpool Football Club was one of the dominating teams in that era, and most of the players were British. It was not the most academic football, but it was entertaining, and the enthusiasm in the stands was amazing. And so was the traditional singing of *YNWA* (*You'll*

Never Walk Alone) from Gerry and the Pacemakers, by the Liverpool Kop. This, undoubtedly was, and is, the most moving soccer chant of all time.

> ***But not all chants were sensitive or gentle; football supporters are not best known for their gentleness, and good manners.***

If supporters were dissatisfied with the quality of the game and specifically if they felt that the opponents were playing in a negative and overly defensive way, they would express their dissatisfaction by shouting out, '*What a Load of Rubbish*'! In fact, when home supporters were not happy with the performance of their own team and specifically with the manager of the club, they sometimes sang it as well.

I remember the word, *rubbish*, because around that time on ITV television station, there was an advertisement campaign running on PG Tips teabags with dressed up chimpanzees. Today, this would be absolutely impossible because animal rights activists would, rightly so, campaign heavily against it. This goes to show how things have evolved. With a bit of luck, you could still find some of these commercials on the internet.

They all, more or less, followed the same script: the chimps were doing something that went a little wrong, but they could then relax with a nice cup of tea. In the one I remember the most, the chimps were redecorating a room, whilst their mum sat in a comfortable chair in the middle of the room observing the work being done. At some point, one of the young chimps looked at her and asked: "*What do you think of it so far, mum?*" She, enjoying her cup of tea, looked up and replied: "*Rubbish!*" It was hilariously funny, but of course, you had to see it to appreciate how funny it was.

It did engrave the word "rubbish" in my long term memory. And every now and then, it pops up in my head, and very often, it is while I am listening to management presentations.

It often amazes me how people can make completely contradictory statements within one speech, and sometimes even within one sentence, and nobody seems to notice.

Generally, these are clichés that sound nice, and are automatically accepted without any further thought. The saying is, of course: *behind every cliché, there is some truth, so maybe I am just too critical or sensitive, but do judge for yourself.*

A very popular statement in relation to change management is: *'The only one who welcomes change is a wet baby.'* Generally, the sentence is on a slide, accompanied by a little drawing of a crying baby that urgently needs its wet diaper replaced.

Funny enough, this slide is typically used in presentations that talk about the ever increasing speed of change. Now this is something that keeps getting me puzzled every time I see or hear it. Basically, the following claim is made: *'Everything is changing extremely rapidly and no one wants it, except wet babies.'* Or putting it differently: the world is run by wet babies. Perhaps parents of young children will nod in agreement, but the entire business community?

Each time I hear it, I notice a majority of the audience, mainly highly educated people, being fully agreeable with it. I was so annoyed with it once that in the question-and-answer section of a presentation, I asked who in the audience was against change. No one raised their hand, so the conclusion had to be: *people are against change, except wet babies and the ones present in this room*. Is this not an amazing coincidence that the only two hundred adults in the world not being against change, had all gathered in that room for that speech? What are the odds?

Beware of statements that contain the word, *people*. Politicians use it a lot and when they use it, it gets the added underlying meaning that all people think the same, which they do not, and that they all want the same as the politician just stated, which they definitely do not.

Politicians are a too-easy target, so I will give you another example. At some point in time, we (at the factory that I once worked for) were faced with a high increase in production. A luxury problem, of course, but it required hiring new people to run our machines in more shifts. The problem was, pretty much like it is today, there were not enough technically schooled people available on the job market. These are the people who, in secondary school, learn a trade and know how to work, not just with their minds, but also with their hands. We were specifically looking for machine operators, but at the same time, we required electrical and mechanical maintenance people, and their like.

In a staff meeting of some thirty people, we were discussing the issue and trying to come up with ways to deal with the problem. The personnel manager made a comment, or rather, more a complaint, saying *"People do not send their children to trade schools anymore,"* implying they should. Everyone in the room agreed. I have no children, so it was difficult for me to relate to the statement, but I did a little survey by asking the simple question as to which of them had children in a trade school. It turned out that only one out of the entire group (of which about twenty-five had children) actually did.

So they all agreed that other people should send their children to trade school, but of course, their own children should go to university.

You would not want them to work with their hands, would you?

There is still a strong tendency to look down on people who work with their hands. I have never understood that, but of course I come from a working-class family. All my family members made a living out of working with their hands. In fact, these are the people that keep society going. How long would we last if there was no one to collect our rubbish, fill the stores with food, or grow and process that food in the first place? What if there were no nurses taking care of our sick and elderly family members, no cleaning ladies to keep our houses clean or crèches looking after our children, so we can go to work and make money?

During a break of an open Six Sigma Green Belt course, one of the participants talked about an experience he had during his student days. At that time he was making some extra money as a waiter in a bar in Knokke, Belgium. For non-Belgians: Knokke is the poshest seaside resort we have. It is the place where the rich and famous gather.

A customer ordered an Irish coffee that the bar had advertised with a picture showing three distinct layers on top of one another: whiskey, coffee and cream. So our waiter goes off to make it, and then brings it to the guest. The customer looks at it, sees there is a little mixing between the layers, and sends the waiter back to make another one because this one was not good enough. The same thing happened with the second coffee. By now, our poor young student gets a little nervous and annoyed, but the customer is king so he prepares a third.

Rather anxious, he presents the third Irish coffee, the customer has a good look at it, says it is fine, takes his spoon and starts stirring the drink until the layers are nicely mixed. In a situation like that, it must take a lot of self-control not to strangle the customer.

Belgian singer Stromae released a song, titled "Santé," which is a word that even people with little knowledge of French will understand. In the song he raises his glass and offers a toast to those who do not have a glass to raise and cannot toast back, because they are busy working: serving people, cleaning toilets, making food, and washing the dishes. They work with low pay, and hear nothing other than complaints from customers and managers alike.

Listen to the song and take his advice: show some more respect to the people who actually make your lifestyle possible.

A young engineer starts in his first job and reports for duty, asking the plant manager what he wants him to do. The plant manager, being very busy, looks up to the new employee and says: "*Well, you can start by sweeping the floor. There is a brush in the corner there.*"

The engineer looks at him amazed, and replies: "*I have studied at the university for five years, surely that is not a job for me!*"

The plant manager then concludes: *"Ah, you are right, in that case, I better show you how to use a brush first."*

We study a lot, but of course, in the end, we still know very little, and should be humble enough to accept that. I worked at the university for a couple of years, and my professor, the late Prof Dr Dilewijns, had a saying related to the point above: *"The easiest way to kill a young engineer is to do exactly as he says."* Act a little arrogant and operators may not warn you of the risks associated with your proposed change. If this leads to a costly mistake, it will not help your career.

Opposing a change may actually be a very positive thing.

It could avoid disaster and prove vital for the success, and even the long-term survival of a company. I know this is another example of a possibility without a probability (see Column 2), but I want to oppose the current thinking that all changes are, by definition, good. Whereas change as such is meaningless, only improvement has value. Not all proposed, and/or more often imposed changes, are an improvement.

In fact, no change is ever an improvement for everything or everyone. There are bound to be negative aspects, sometimes for the business process as a whole, but as good as always for at least some of the people that are active in the process being changed. Not having the openness of mind to listen to rightful comments is one of the reasons for resistance to change.

People continually go through major changes in their lives: they study, look for a job, change jobs, get into a relationship, start a family, buy a house and so on. They can make drastic, life-changing decisions, make investments of hundreds of thousands of Euros, and raise children, but when they are working for you they are said to be *resistant to change*. Could it not be that the problem lies more with you than with them?

If people were resistant to change, we would all still live in caves. But the changes people make have two characteristics: they have decided on the change themselves, and it implies an improvement to their lives. With that in mind, you do not have to spend fortunes on the change management industry: involve the people in developing the change, listen to their comments, and take them seriously. Simple rules will get you a long way.

Being fashionable is another important aspect of management. Not in the clothes you wear, but in the systems you use. So, when the term, *diversification*, was launched many years ago, no one could stay behind. It sounded like an interesting idea, and the word had a nice ring to it, slightly academic, but it was still understandable. There is also a logic in it: if you are good at making cars, why would you not be good at running hotels? There are probably a hundred reasons why you would not be good at running hotels, but why would you listen to negative people who are against change? So, let us diversify, and show we are in line with modern business thinking.

Unfortunately, not all diversifications turned out to be great successes. Even negative people are right sometimes. The problem is: can we admit that we failed at diversification? Probably not! In fact, what organisation would ever admit to a failure of any kind?

As a result, you are stuck in a tricky situation, until someone comes up with a new, interestingly sounding approach: *'Focus on your core business.'* Basically, this is going 100% in the opposite of diversification, but it is the ideal way out. There is no longer a need to say you have failed, you can confirm once more that you are always in line with the most modern management thinking.

Focusing on the core business has automatically led to outsourcing on a large scale, and one of the sectors that has done that very extensively is the automotive industry. Complete systems have been outsourced to such an extent that most of the value of a car is produced by suppliers, and the knowledge on these systems is held by those respective suppliers. The reasoning was that this was the most profitable way to produce cars.

Today, there is huge concern in the European automotive industry about the competition from Chinese car makers, and specifically, in the production of electric cars. Even Tesla is experiencing problems in the Chinese market because the local competition is technically and economically very fierce.

In the economic pages of a Belgian newspaper, a comment was published about this topic. One of the reasons mentioned for the success of Chinese car makers was that they had over 75% of the value chain in their own hands. In other words, because they outsourced very little they are the most competitive. So much for focusing on your core business. Just like with diversification, not all outsourcing had good results or was a good idea to start with. But it was heavily promoted, at the time, in the same economic pages.

A builder of agricultural equipment announced that it will carry out a thorough outsourcing programme and management said that this would greatly reduce costs. About two years later, the same management announced they would start to insource several parts, because that would greatly reduce costs.

One of the engineers at the meeting listened very carefully and he came up with a suggestion: *"What if we were to do this outsourcing/insourcing a couple more times? With a bit of luck, we can end up getting the parts for free."* His improvement idea was not very well received by management, even though it did contain some logic.

In Column 2, I referred to the often-used LinkedIn quote about people not being here to be average, but to be awesome. Apart from the comments I made there, I have to admit that being awesome and leading an awesome life is probably amazing. I have no idea, I just wonder if it is not tiring to always have to be awesome or passionate, because that is also very popular today; we need to be passionate about what we are doing. I am lazy by birth and principle, so just having to think about being passionate in everything I do, makes me feel tired already.

Not only do you need to be passionate about work, but you also have to be passionate about your family and passionate about your hobbies. At some point in time, that barrel of passion must be empty, and then at the bottom, you will find a burn-out.

As a side issue: the value of laziness is grossly underestimated in business.

For some reason, people admire hard work, but generally, hard work is needed because half of the time, things have to be done twice. We work hard to correct previous mistakes, being busy with the past. Whereas laziness is a key driver of innovation, and by thinking about what to do to even be lazier, you are creating the future.

As a consultant, I was supporting an improvement team in a print shop with the objective to increase productivity. One of the workers made a proposal involving changes to individual jobs, as well as reorganisation of the flow of material. It looked like a sound plan to me, so I proposed to run a test for a couple of weeks, and to evaluate the test results afterwards. The plant manager was a bit doubtful, but as I, an expensive external consultant, approved it, he allowed the test to go through.

At the following meeting, the results were evaluated; productivity had improved beyond the original project objective and the operators could work much more relaxed. Success all over, you would think, but the plant manager was not fully convinced.

In a private conversation with me, he expressed his concern. He had to admit the results were beyond expectation but, *"People seem so much at ease at their workplace, and they do not give the impression of working hard."*

It was as if he preferred to see the input of hard work over the output of smart work.

Believe me, when things are hectic and everyone is running around, people may be working hard, but they will not be very productive. Perhaps a little more balance would not be a bad thing. Maybe we would even perform better by not being overly passionate about our job.

In the famous novel, "Anna Karenina," by Lev Tolstoy, the character, Stepan Arkadjevitsj Oblonski (I love classical Russian novels and the fantastic names of the characters) is praised for being really good at his job. His secret to that, Tolstoy writes, is that he could not care less about what he was doing. As a consequence, the decisions he took were not clouded by feelings or passions, and tended to be objective and the right ones.

Now you may say this is fiction, but David O'Leary, the chief executive officer (CEO) of Ryanair, said something fairly similar. He noticed all his competitor CEOs were passionate about planes and flying, and that made them make wrong decisions. He, on the other hand, could not care less: a plane is a flying bus, taking people from destination A to B, and the only thing that matters is how to get that done as cost-efficiently as possible.

I never fly Ryanair. I do not like the way they treat their personnel or their customers. But you cannot deny the business success of the company, so maybe being a little less passionate might not be a bad idea, as a manager. Also, leading a little more balanced life might not be a bad idea, as a human being.

The extremely high number of burn-outs these days shows us there are limits to all that passion.

So often, the problem lies in the words we use. For whatever reason, we seem to need superlatives. Work is important, and takes up a lot of your time, so it is a very good idea to do things you like doing. It is equally important to do them well, but you do not necessarily have to be passionate about it. After all, it is just work.

There is a nice story about Laurence Olivier, the famous British actor. One of his co-actors in a film had a scene where he had to arrive on stage out of breath. To prepare, he ran up and down some stairs a couple of times so when the scene started, he would actually be out of breath. Olivier looked at him in amazement while he was running back and forth and asked: "*Why do you not just act?*"

Modern professional life is no joke: not only do they want you to be passionate, but you also have to leave your comfort zone! So, just when you are about to master your job, the moment you know more or less what you are doing or are supposed to be doing, they assign you to another job.

Being a football fanatic, this has always puzzled me, because in football the total opposite is valid: never change a winning team! Imagine a coach getting players out of their comfort zone: Cristiano Ronaldo in goal, Lionel Messi at left-back, Robert Lewandowski as defensive midfielder and Thibaut Courtois as striker. Why on earth would you do that? What good could come out of that?

You do not want people to get *rusty* on a job, but getting them out of their comfort zone for the fun of it, is not a good idea.

People who feel comfortable have less stress, are more confident, and offer more value.

Jobs are also getting increasingly more complicated, require a high level of expertise and take more time to master. You do not want to throw that knowledge away, just like you do not want Cristiano Ronaldo in goal. Besides, consultants who tell companies to get their employees out of their comfort zone, tend to do that for years in a row. Should that not ring a bell?

Who works for you is of course your choice, and some years ago, I heard a keynote speaker tell the audience that as a leader, hiring staff was important but very simple: *"You have to surround yourself with the best people."*

As usual, everyone nodded, while I shook my head. There must be something terribly wrong with me, because for some reason, I always see problems. Whereas, according to modern management theory, there are no problems, only opportunities! So, why do I not detect them? In fact, you may wonder, what could possibly be wrong with surrounding yourself with the best people?

Well, for one, how do you define best? People are complex creatures with many characteristics, so what amazing features would an accountant need to have, for you to hire them as '*The best*?'

Great in accounting work undoubtedly, with several years of experience, a team player, a good communicator and maybe some other aspects you find important for an accountant. Having defined the criteria you can look for that perfect accountant and hire the person. Great for you.

But now I need an accountant for my company, and I am in serious trouble. The best accountant is no longer available on the job market as he/she works for you now, so I need to settle for second best. If I am fast enough that is, otherwise, it will be third, fourth, etc.

It is pretty simple: there is no way you will ever be able to surround yourself with the best people. And think about what will happen if your super accountant is taken out of his comfort zone and then appointed as head of engineering.

A good company is not good because it has the best people. Like all other companies, it has people of different skills, talents, characters and levels.

What makes a company special is that it is able to do extraordinary things with ordinary people.

By the way, it may sound nice that you have to surround yourself with the best people, but most people do not decide who surrounds them.

On social media, you regularly read slogans telling you not to surround yourself with negative people. As if you would have much control over that. At work, you cannot control that unless you are the CEO, and even then it has its limits. You will have to work with the colleagues you get, the positive and the negative ones. Looking for a company where only positive people work is an alternative, but I fear you would be unemployed for a very long time then.

This even goes beyond the workplace. You may find your brother-in-law to be a useless, energy-draining jerk, and you may be right, but he comes with your partner. You can decide never to accompany your partner on family visits, but in the long run that will not have a positive effect on your relationship.

In real life, things are much more complex than what is displayed on social media posts. You will need to cope with many things you do not like. But hey, we all have to make a living.

COLUMN 5
TEAMWORK

I don't want to compete with anyone; I
hope we all make it.
Facebook Quote

To visit a supplier in Sheffield, United
Kingdom, we (one of our purchasers and
myself) took the night ferry from
Zeebrugge to Hull. On arrival, a sales
representative of the supplier picked us up and
drove us to their factory. As we entered the
town, he announced our arrival in a loud voice:

*"Welcome to Sheffield, where the
birds fly backwards to avoid the
dirt in their eyes."*

This was 1988, and at that time it was no longer
true, birds no longer flew backwards in
Sheffield. However, it did sum up the history of
the entire region.

Sheffield, at the heart of the Industrial
Revolution, was very rich and highly populated.
Gradually, due to international competition, it
began to lose its key industrial position, and
this led to it becoming poor. Backed by a
service-driven economy, it was renovated,

growing, and flourishing again in the twenty-first (21st) century. It is, to some extent, representative of the evolution of the Western economy as a whole.

I remember this, because only two years later, I went back to the region, this time to Birmingham, for one of the famous 3½-day seminars held by Dr W Edwards Deming. This was probably also one of the last seminars he gave. It was certainly a unique opportunity, and I am very glad I was able to attend it. I learnt a lot, and had some nice encounters with interesting people.

Of course, at that time, Dr Deming was 90 years old, and it was clear that lecturing at these seminars was very tiring to him. He started the course in the morning with some gym exercises, and a theoretical session based on his fourteen points for Western management, as described in his book *'Out Of The Crisis'*. At the end of each day, he returned for a brief question-and-answer (Q&A) session. During the day, his assistants kept us busy with group exercises. Of the many things I recall from that course, two points stand out.

At the first Q&A session, one of the participants asked the following (rather daring) question: *"Dear Dr Deming, thank you very much for giving this course. However, what on earth makes you come to Birmingham, England, of all places, to talk about quality management at the age of 90? Your reputation as a guru is well established, and you probably do not need the money, so why do you do this?"*

Dr Deming waited a little, thinking, and then replied:

"Well, you never know I might learn something."

Very wise words, and perhaps the ultimate definition of age: as long as you can start the day with the idea that you might learn something, you are young; at least, at heart.

The second thing I remember was something he said while talking about numerical quotas, goals and measuring people, in general. As an example of the detrimental effect of ranking people, he referred to a festival where children could participate in a drawing contest. They were all being very creative and enjoying themselves until the result of the contest was announced. Three children were now very happy, but all the others were rather sad because they had lost. Deming's main message was that life is not, and should never be, a contest or a game, and that we should work together to make things better for everyone, more or less in line with the Facebook quote shown in the subtitle above. In more statistical terms: move the entire distribution to a higher level.

A couple of years later, I heard a totally different story, but its meaning was quite similar. It was told by a teacher from the United Kingdom who went to the outback of Australia to teach Aboriginal children. It was her contribution to making the world a better place to live in, and to reach out to those who were left behind. She talked about the first lesson in physical education she gave.

Her idea was to start with something very simple: a running contest. She pointed to a tree and said to the children, *"We will have a running contest. At the count of three, you all start running to that tree over there, and the one who arrives first is the winner."*

The children looked at her, seemingly confused, and one replied: *"But then all the others are losers, why would we do that?"*

That statement startled her, but nonetheless she persisted: *"Well, to see who is the fastest, who is the best in running."*

That did not convince the children so they discussed amongst themselves and concluded:

"We will walk hand-in-hand to that tree all together. That is much more fun, and then nobody loses. So, off they went."

Now, how cool is that? In business, we would call this a self-directed team, literally even in this case.

However, I am not sure if many CEOs would be happy with the solution chosen. They tend to promote teamwork with words, but I suspect that deep down they prefer competition. In fact, many of them tend to stimulate competition internally.

One of the best examples of this is found in the automotive industry, where the real competitor for the employees is not another brand, but the other factories within the same brand. Factories fight against each other to decide who will be allowed to build the next model. At the same time, we expect that people will exchange their knowledge in internal benchmarking with their most fierce and feared competitors. Is it not amazing that top managers can be so naive? The last ones employees will tell anything interesting to, will be their competitor colleagues of other factories. Can you blame them?

Nevertheless, we spend quite a lot of money organising team building exercises and events. A customer once requested that I evaluate the functioning of their design and development department. The first step was to talk to the people (mainly engineers) and to hear their views and ideas on the strengths and weaknesses of the department as well as its processes. During lunch break, some talked about a team-building weekend in the Belgian Ardennes, which had been organised by the personnel department.

It had been announced with some pomp and circumstance. It was going to bring people together, improve teamwork and create a better atmosphere at work. That would in turn lead to higher quality and productivity in every department, including in the engineering department. To say the least, these are indeed high expectations. Most people at the meeting were very enthusiastic about it, and it was clear that they were eager to join the weekend.

However, there was one guy who was a bit hesitant, and indicated he was unsure if he would go. This hesitancy was definitely brave, because even if it was not compulsory, the company expectations and social pressure to attend were high. The others did not understand his hesitation at all and asked why. He made his reservations clear with the following statement: "*Well, I would like to go, but I doubt very much if this will really lead to all these amazing improvements at work that are announced.*" Everyone at the table burst into laughter following this rather serious statement.

"*Of course not,*" one said, "*...we all know this will not change much. But it will be a lot of fun with walks in the woods, and good meals and lots of beer in the evenings. And all paid for by the company! You must be mad to let that skip. Do you really believe any of us take that personnel department talk serious?*"

It was both funny, and a bit sad at the same time.

The only person who was seriously evaluating the perceived goals of the weekend, was not taken seriously.

In hindsight, being an outside observer with a bad character, I must admit I mainly found it funny. There is nothing wrong with group events and team-building exercises, but stay realistic in your expectations. Climbing hills or building rafts will not, in itself, improve the company's quality. Having a good time together is nice enough as an objective.

Outside of the business world, there are many benchmarks of teamwork to be found. As you already have read in some of the previous columns, I am a big football fan, and I truly love the game.

In one of the episodes of the brilliant "Inspector Morse" television series, the down-to-earth Sergeant Lewis talked about his father in this interesting statement: *"My father loved football, but he did not like football players."* This was because he found football players to be quite arrogant, hopelessly egocentric and ridiculously overpaid. These are characteristics that have only exponentially increased since. Morse's reply was: *"Your father, Lewis, was a wise man. He saw the difference between what people do and who they really are."*

As if all this arrogance and egocentricity do not make it difficult enough, football teams have other characteristics that are often seen as highly problematic in society. They are multicultural and multi-generational, with a mix of young and older players. But despite all of that, you can see amazing teamwork in football teams. Just like in business, they have a manager and different players with different skills playing together to achieve a team goal. I do not want to say that all football teams function perfectly, but given all the negatives, many of them function exceptionally well. Can we learn something from why it is so?

There are a couple of things that make teamwork in sports easier. First of all, there is a very clear goal, and it is the same for all players: winning! Everyone in the team contributes to that goal directly and gets continuous feedback on the situation. That feedback is at a team level, but also on an individual level: are we winning, and am I playing well?

Getting this double and immediate feedback is extremely motivating. This is especially so, because the success of the team is automatically positive for each player, as it increases their market value. There is a huge feeling of belonging to, and taking part in the success (and failure) of the team, for each individual.

This actually reveals another interesting aspect of teamwork:

There is no such thing as a team that works, only individual people do.

And that is the manager's task during the week: preparing individual players in such a way that their individual performance will make the team better when it is game time. There are technical and tactical elements to it, but the crux of the matter is that it all depends on the manager's people management skills.

Having said that, when the moment of truth arrives at game time, it is to a very large extent, down to the players. One could even say that the work of the manager almost stops when the game begins. He can observe and intervene, but he is extremely dependent on his players. He has to make sure that they are well prepared, physically, tactically and mentally, because now it is no longer in his hands. This is a lesson in modesty for all managers!

Now, like players, football managers are not the most modest of people. Many observers, journalists and analysts attribute them mythical powers, so it is probably not easy to stay modest. When a team struggles and risks relegation (a fate worse than death in professional football), the standard reaction is to replace the manager. This is a logical decision in view of the presumed impact, but it could be a rather costly one, and remarkably, very rarely successful: all data show that teams that replace their manager do not increase their chances of avoiding relegation.

But if failure is not determined by the manager, surely creating success must be? Well, not really; a study on the results of

English Premier League football teams between 2003 and 2012 showed that there was a 90% correlation between their success and players' wage expenditure. In other words, the team with the highest paid players (read: the best players) generally wins, regardless of the manager.

To have the relationship between the players and their manager working well, there must be mutual trust and respect. In football, as a manager you have to let go, but in business, there is a lot of micro-management, because managers still want to play themselves. They want to show off how good they are in things that are no longer part of their actual job. What they should be doing is making others better.

In order to make it clear that people are capable of doing their own jobs properly without having a manager observing their every move, the term "empowerment" was invented.

For some reason, business leaders always need a fancy word to understand the plain obvious.

All those years ago, CEOs all over the world had this amazing revelation: *people who do a job eight hours a day actually know what they are doing*. Who would have ever thought that? Not that the consequences were accepted that easily or that it was all properly implemented. There is a cultural element, of course; sadly, trust in employees is sometimes very low.

An airline company once had serious grievances about the way they handled customer complaints when something went wrong whilst serving in-flight meals. A typical example of this is when food or drink is spilled on a customer during the flight, leaving them with stains on their clothes.

They had a system: a form needed to be filled out, and sent to a central administrative department, which handled the case by giving the customer the approval to charge costs. To be reimbursed, a detailed receipt of cleaning costs had to be sent back, which had to be checked and approved (we clearly do not trust customers either) by the same department. Once all that had gone well, some three months later, the customer eventually received their refund of claimed costs.

To do something about the complaints regarding this procedure, a member of staff made a remarkably simple proposal: let us give the people on the plane the authority to talk to the customer and agree on an amount for compensation that they can then pay immediately. The company knew what the average costs were, so basically, it was not that difficult for a flight attendant to judge the costs associated with any specific case. If the customer did not accept the proposal, they could still complete the form and go through the regular lengthy procedure.

This idea was proposed by the personnel manager at a directors' meeting, and all hell broke loose. How on earth could anyone propose that a flight attendant be given authority to decide how to spend company money? Obviously, if given the chance, and with no one controlling them, these people would waste it to excess. It sounded as if the directors actually thought flight attendants would start pouring wine and food on customers' clothing just to be able to spend huge amounts of company funds. So much for mutual trust and respect!

Nevertheless, the personnel manager insisted and asked if it would not be possible to just start with a small test to see how it went. After a lot of back-and-forth discussions, the proposal was finally agreed. The test worked well, customers were very satisfied with the process, and the total cost of the programme became relatively lower than it had been before.

Let us get back to teamwork and ask ourselves why it would not work. Deliberately creating internal competition rather than cooperation is one cause, as discussed above. Misalignment of goals is another one. You see it in football teams when a player is looking for a lucrative transfer. Now, his goal is no longer to win, but to avoid tackles and the risk of getting injured.

In that case, teams simply do not succeed. You see it in sports, and you see it in international political gatherings.

A typical example is the several COP (Conference of the Parties) meetings on climate change that have been held for years. By the time this book gets published, the 28th will have been finished, and I am fairly confident that, like the previous 27, it will not lead to any real breakthrough. The common goal is as clear as a football team's goal: keep the global rise of world temperature below two degrees centigrade (2.0°C), and preferably below 1.5°C, as compared to pre-industrial times.

Some of these COP meetings have been called historical. The best known have led to the Kyoto Protocol in 1997 and the Paris Agreement in 2015.

But despite all the nice words and the historic agreements, there has been a steady increase in CO_2 concentration in the atmosphere. In my more cynical moments, I refer to the COP meetings as proof that net zero does exist: you can gather for almost thirty years in a row, and end with zero results.

Why? Because the participating players, in this case, the parties, all enter the pitch with different interests and individual objectives that they want to defend. When these are put above the team goal, results rarely follow.

COLUMN 6
COMPANY CULTURE

Culture Eats Strategy for Breakfast
Peter Drucker

Anthropology is the knowledge area that deals with the study of human societies, cultures and their development. Very few people in quality have any background on this subject. In all those years in quality, I only once met a quality specialist, in this case, a Six Sigma Master Black Belt, who also had a degree in anthropology. This is really an interesting combination, and one that ought to be promoted a bit more in quality, and in management in general, just like psychology. After all, quality management is, like any form of management, first and foremost, people management.

I am not a professional anthropologist, but on the other hand, neither was Peter Drucker, and that did not stop him from saying what has been quoted as the subtitle for this Column. In fact, there are several variations on that quote.

The first one I ever heard was, *"Culture eats process for lunch every day."* A different dish and meal, but the same meaning: *nothing beats culture*! I would not dare challenge Peter Drucker, but the question is: *how do we define culture, and more specifically, company culture?*

One Sunday evening, I watched three separate documentaries in a row, and they all mentioned culture in some way or another. The first one was from the series "Treasures of the World," and it talked about ancient Greek cities with a special attention to Sparta. The culture of Sparta is mythical: based on discipline, very militarised and with the golden rule that the city, the community, are always more important than its individual citizens. It contains very little to zero compassion, and often borders on cruelty, so it should not be idealised. However, the notion that the whole, the global result, is more important than the individual objectives, is interesting when thinking about a company culture.

It is very much embedded in Japanese culture and subsequently, seen in the way Japanese organisations operate. I asked a quality manager, who had worked in the automotive industry for European and Japanese manufacturers, what was so special about Japanese company culture.

He immediately replied: less management ego.

This did not mean that there was no status attached to the different layers in an organization, but the ego of a manager never stood in the way of the best possible solution for the overall project. I got a similar comment from a friend who worked for a European and a Japanese car manufacturer. In both cases, he was involved in projects for new car models, making the link between the product design and the process design development phases. His observation was that the first prototype drawings and specifications in both cases had loads of problems from a manufacturability point of view. Process engineering then made an extensive report with a myriad of proposed changes that was sent back to the product developers.

When the second revised prototype drawings arrived, a clear difference could be noted. Japanese product designers had considered all remarks and changed the design as much as possible in order to help process engineering and the manufacturing process. Where that was not possible, they clearly explained why, and worked with their pre-production colleagues to jointly come to a final solution.

A possible explanation could be that the Japanese product designers always thought about the overall impact of the new car project on the success of the company. Changing the design so that the part can be produced or assembled easier and cheaper is a plus for the overall project and shared goals, therefore, it needs to be done wherever possible.

Their European counterparts ignored many of the remarks and left the product design to a large extent unchanged. Perhaps their ego was too big to accept comments from others. They preferred to stick with their personal design over a solution that could be better for the project. They left it up to the process engineers to find a way to produce and/or assemble the parts as best as possible, given their, undoubtedly brilliant, design. This example shows that culture has an impact on even the smallest technical detail of a specific part. No wonder it is more important than the process.

Peter Drucker is the father of *management by objectives*, a theory that was clearly in contrast with W Edwards Deming, who aimed for *"The elimination of numerical quotas for the workforce and numerical goals for management."* It is fair to say that Drucker won the battle, and today, we generally express the objectives as Key Performance Indicators

(KPIs). Very often, the indicators are turned into departmental goals, local KPIs that become critical for the manager involved (and their bonus).

Studying a process that involved several departments in a fairly large company, an improvement team came up with a proposal that would improve the product flow through the entire process chain. However, the team members themselves gave the proposal little to no chance of being accepted; the proposed reorganisation would cause some of the departments involved to see a negative impact on their KPIs.

There is no way that any manager would accept that kind of change, even if it was for the good of the company.

Remuneration and various types of reward systems are also an expression of company culture with a clear impact on behaviour, and as the above example shows, it is not always for the best of the organisation. Perhaps Deming was right after all!

Returning to my television documentaries on the Sunday evening referred to above: the next one I watched came from the series on great American railroads by the inimitable

Michael Portillo. In this episode, he travelled on the Trans-Canadian railroad from Vancouver to Toronto. On one of his first stops, he spoke with some representatives of the Canadian First Nations, as they are called today. It was, and it is still, a sad story of a culture that had almost been eradicated in a most brutal way, as recent discoveries of mass graves of children have shown once more. It is yet another example of how thinking in terms of cultural superiority can lead to the most horrible acts of cruelty.

Nevertheless, the culture of the First Nations has survived. It is based on respect for all living beings, highly spiritual, and focused on nature. We talk a lot about sustainability these days, and many systems are developed to report on its level in an organisation. All are very technical, and often accounting-like, with ESG (Environmental, Social and Governance) and EU CSRD (European Union Corporate Sustainability Reporting Directive) as some of the best-known and utmost influential examples.

These systems require a lot of effort, but do not always result in a high return on sustainability. Return, of course, being a more sustainable organisation. All the energy sapped by reporting no longer becomes available for making improvements. In particular, small and medium-sized organisations may have no energy left after reporting.

Besides, if we want to take care of planet Earth's biosphere and avoid catastrophes, the time for reporting is long gone, action is what is needed. To be successful in that action, we will need the right culture. This must include respect for all living things, and genuine care for the natural environment.

So, without over-romanticising the First Nations culture, it could be an interesting source of inspiration if a sustainability-driven organisational culture is what you are aiming for. Maybe, if we had learned a little from their culture instead of trying to eradicate it, we would not be in this anthropocentric age of serious biodiversity collapse and climate change.

The last documentary I watched on that day was from the series "Extreme Lands," and it talked about the impact of global warming on California. The program focused on preserving water and reducing greenhouse gas exhausts. There was also an intriguing remark on culture by one of the people interviewed. He mentioned an important aspect that needed to be taken into account.

"We see it as a right to use as much energy as we want, like driving big cars. It is in our culture."

This is not quite in line with First Nations thinking, but it was something that came to my attention back in 1986, when I travelled to the United States of America for the first time. It was a work visit, and the company had arranged a rental car for me to pick up on arrival at the airport. I collected a Buick, which was a very nice and comfortable car, and about twice the size of the car I was driving at home. It took some getting used to.

Things have changed since then. Now there are hardly any car drivers left in the USA, most have become truck drivers. That resembles Europe where people now drive SUVs (Sports Utility Vehicles). They are heavily promoted by car manufacturers, and in advertisements, you will read that with an SUV, you can get anywhere and more specifically, to places that have no roads to them. It feels like great relief, but 95% of these cars will never be driven on anything other than concrete roads.

With a lot of thanks to technological improvements, car engines have become more fuel-efficient. However, this clear trend has completely been turned around because of the push for bigger and heavier cars. One could say that consumers and producers together, have successfully annihilated the progress made by engineers in engine efficiency over the last thirty years – quite an achievement. This is not to mention the increased risk of serious accidents with heavier cars. You cannot beat the laws of physics; brake distance becomes longer with weight. You are undoubtedly safer in your big car; the risk lies with all the others, specifically, pedestrians and cyclists.

As you can see, culture can mean a lot of different things, from iron discipline to spirituality, and burning gasoline. Returning to the Peter Drucker statement and its variants, both strategy and process can be clearly stated and communicated. Culture, however, is less tangible. Some companies attempt to express culture by defining company values. This is probably the closest you can get to having statements written down on company culture, and this text can be as easily communicated as strategy. However, the text is not the culture.

What is actually happening, what is being done, how are people treated; those are expressions of culture. It is in the acts, not in the words; but if you choose words, make sure to act accordingly.

For some time, it was rather popular to state that '*People are our most important asset.*' This sounds nice, but as soon as the financial results were not as good as expected, the first action was very often to lay off people. When in trouble, getting rid of your most important asset must be about the dumbest thing anyone can do. Putting it differently: it quickly became clear that people only were the most important asset in words, not in reality.

Car companies often talk about their care for the environment, and today, this is one of the most used advertisement arguments, and as part of their mission, vision and value statements.

Martin Winterkorn was forced to resign as the CEO of Volkswagen as a result of the Dieselgate scandal. His company had programmed certain diesel engine driven cars to only activate their emission controls during laboratory emissions testing. In that way, they misled authorities (and consumers) all over the world about their real impact on air quality. When it was discovered, it turned out that the actual NOx[2] exhaust in real-world driving was

---

[2] NOx – this is what can be referred to as *nitrogen oxides*, which is said to be a most relevant cause for air pollution.

forty times higher than what was shown during testing.

Winterkorn, as the CEO, was adjudged to have ultimate responsibility, but it is highly unlikely – a massive understatement in itself – that he wrote the software himself. Many people worked on it, they knew about it, tested it and carried out improvements on it. They all, knowingly, went against company values, demonstrating other values that clearly mattered more to the company and to them. I can even imagine that some of the people were rather proud of what they had technically achieved. After all, this had worked perfectly for many years. This example shows that not sticking to values is not necessarily a vice of top management alone.

A very important aspect of culture is that it denotes an all-encompassing system that influences all results achieved. Comparing one element, or just one result without taking into account the associated cultural system, is bound to lead to false conclusions. This is an error that is very often made when comparing results, like in benchmarking.

Just to give one example: in a large multi-national organisation a benchmarking project was started to compare maintenance costs. A company that had recently been taken over, was told by head office that the study revealed they had *"excessive maintenance costs,"* compared to other units within the group.

One thing the accountants had not looked at was the degree of technicality of the various units with, of course, a serious effect on maintenance cost.

However, even when comparing with similar units, their maintenance cost was still rather high. To learn and improve, they paid to visit to a factory that the study had identified as the benchmark for this aspect of the business. The visit confirmed the factory indeed had a lower maintenance cost but when other results were compared, it also became clear it had a significantly lower productivity. This was mainly due to equipment breakdown. Cherry picking generally leads to wrong conclusions for the simple reason that things are linked and interact.

At one of the conferences organised by the American Society for Quality, I heard an interesting definition of company culture.

Culture is what people do when they are not told what to do.

Do people constantly need instructions to do what is expected? Does performance depend on continual control and observation? Are they not to be trusted, or do you not trust them? If that is the case, people will not be proactive, as they will be hesitant and wait for an order before doing anything. You get what you give – if you do not trust your people, they will not trust you; if you do not respect others, you will not be respected, and so on. Make no mistake: people will listen to what you say, but they will mainly observe what you do, and how they are being treated. They know whether or not you are sincere.

In Belgium, when you are ill and cannot go to work, you must go to a doctor to obtain a sick note. A professional confirmation that you are what you claim to be: unfit to work. In many cases, that is a waste of time, yours and the doctors', and a waste of money, yours and social security's. Besides, by forcing you to go and sit in a packed waiting room, the perfect environment is created to spread even more diseases. Any attempt to change this system has been blocked by employer organisations. And these are generally the same organisations that complain about the high cost of social security.

In Denmark, where some of my family live, they do not know this system. When you are ill, you stay at home until you are well enough to return to work. For several common diseases, paying a visit to a doctor is pointless, and the best thing to do is to rest and wait it out. You call your boss to tell them you are ill, and will return to work when you feel better. The boss believes you.

These different systems have no effect on absenteeism whatsoever. It is not higher in Denmark than in Belgium, the only difference is that Danish employees are trusted, and Belgian employees are not. Consequently, the latter will not trust their employer either. Stating trust as a key value in your value statement is close to ridiculous, and will not be believed by anyone.

A personnel manager of a large organisation once mentioned an observation, that is a good indication of having a positive company culture: "*People that have left us, always speak positively about us.*"

Admittedly, it is a bit late and after the facts, but it shows that people can leave your company without being unhappy working for you. That is why it is so important to have exit talks. It will teach you a lot about your company culture.

The funny thing is that the same personnel manager also mentioned he had no real clue as to why this was so. He could not point to any specific thing they did, except maybe a genuine culture of respect for all.

Treating your personnel as people instead of human resources is a good first step.

Good manners leading to good management and to a good company culture.

COLUMN 7
POLITICS ARE EVERYWHERE

All the world's a stage, and all the men
and women merely players.
William Shakespeare

In July 2013, I was fortunate to visit Uganda, and see mountain gorillas and chimpanzees up close. Both animals live in groups and are male dominated, but there is a big difference between the two. Silver back gorillas are impressive animals, but they are also a kind of gentle giants that feed on plants and ants. Through the entire visit, we had a feeling of calm; there was no moment of anxiety or fear, not even when the animals passed us within just a few meters.

Quite different from the chimpanzees. To begin with, they are noisy, very noisy! You hear them from a long distance away, and getting closer, the noise is truly terrifying. Walking in a forest with chimpanzees around you creates a form of anxiety that is difficult to explain, but feels very real. Chimpanzees are cruel hunters of other monkeys; its underlying aggression can be felt even when they are just observing you calmly from a tree branch.

Chimpanzees are very popular animals that are close to us humans, genetically, and consequently, behaviourally. Many studies have been undertaken about chimpanzee communities, both in the wild and in zoo groups. The latter is, of course, much easier to perform. One specific aspect that always shows up in these studies is the high number of politics within chimpanzee communities. There is a power struggle, coalitions are being made, deceit is visible and so on. Politics seems to be an inherent characteristic of chimpanzees, and subsequently, of people.

After all, we are just apes with an attitude sharing 99% of our DNA with chimps.

Some of us become professional politicians, but we are all political animals; this becomes apparent within any group of people. So it is clearly present in many organisations, because of what an organisation is: a group of people.

A way of expressing power is territory, both in location and size. Companies with large office buildings classically have the offices of their top people located at the highest floor level. They are literally on top of all the others, and as such, clearly recognisable to all as *Chief Chimps*.

Equally important is the space your territory occupies. In a company I worked for, the marketing and engineering offices were situated on the second floor. For whatever reason, the two departments had to switch sides, and as a result, the respective marketing and engineering managers had to swap offices. No big deal, you would say; however, the sales manager insisted on major changes to his 'new' office before making the move. One of the things they had to do was to shift a wall a little so his new office would occupy at least the same surface as his old one. The bigger territory you occupy, the more important you are perceived to be.

Another way of looking (as well as being) powerful is to have a lot of people reporting to you. To hire new people, an agreement from others in the organisation is often required, and that can be difficult when money is tight. It is, therefore, important to hire as many as possible when things are going well, and money is available. Fewer questions are asked, and you can fill up your department, look more important, and have an added benefit that is often forgotten and definitely underestimated: you can shine when things get worse!

Most companies have cyclical behaviour, so after the seven good years come the seven meagre years and cost-cutting follows. Now, your time has come, and your moment of glory has arrived.

'I know how difficult things are, and that we need to cut some 10% of staff, but to show my devotion to this organisation, in my department, I will lay-off 15% of my staff and we will work extra hard to make up for it.' This is the statement of a true management hero, which is not difficult to attain because you were smart enough to be at least 20% overstaffed before the hard times hit.

That is what smart politicians and managers do: foresee what can happen, and take the necessary actions to always look good.

Understanding changes in power is also extremely important to keep or improve your position. In our factory, the CEO announced his retirement and then appointed the financial director as his successor. It was fascinating to see how all of a sudden, no one needed the advice of the current CEO anymore. At the same time, you could see the carpet of his successor's office getting worn out.

It is one thing to get to the top, it is another to stay there, as every sportsman, and every dominant male chimp knows. I once heard a top manager in healthcare say he spent half of his time doing his job and the other half protecting his position.

It reminded me of an older employee I worked with while consulting in their company. During lunch, he told me the following: "*When I started to work here as a young engineer, I really looked up to the top people in the organisation. I thought these people were devoted to the organisation, and did everything they did for it. I truly believed that. However, after all these years, I have learned they are mainly interested in their personal career and personal position.*"

By the way, you find politics at every layer of an organisation. It tends to be most visible at the highest level, but it is everywhere. Emails are a good way of showing how important you are, and some people are very good at it. Programme an email, so it is sent at two o'clock in the morning, showing pretty much everyone (cc is an excellent function) how hard you work and think about the company at all times.

At the beginning of my consulting career, I met a Dutch consultant who pointed out another important issue: it is not about who you are and what you know, but about what people think you are and think you know. It is about the perception people have of you. He also pointed out how easy it was to impress people and to have them believe the perception rather than the reality.

As an example, he gave me his business card, which displayed his title as *Vice-President Europe*. He worked for a US-based consulting firm, and was actually the only employee in Europe, but there is no reason why the only employee could not be the Vice President. In fact, he told me he had wanted to put President on it, but the US company President did not want to see anyone else in the organisation with the same title. His ego could not take that.

Looking important opens doors, looking wise is the next step. He had another lesson for me on the same subject. "*When you are asked to give a quote for a project, and the company shows some interest in working with you, always try to arrange a visit. If they are interested, they will want to see and talk to you anyway. When you are there, ask for a tour of the company premises.*"

These are very logical things to do, and any smart consultant will work that way, but he had an added tip. After the visit, once you return to the office, you can casually drop something like, "…*it seems like a good organisation, but I think communication and motivation could be an issue.*" They will think you are a genius, because within half an hour, and with just taking a tour of the company, you spotted two of their major problems.

> **You cannot go wrong: all companies have a problem with communication and motivation, or at least they think they do.**

I have to admit that I never tried it; I did not have the guts or the nerve, but if any of you consider a career in consulting, you could use it to your advantage.

Perception is everything. As a young quality manager, I was asked by the Chief Executive Officer (CEO) to help prepare him for a major international meeting at the head office. Managers of the various plants would present their five-year plans to the board of directors.

Every manager had to contribute, and I had to prepare a five-year quality plan. It had to have some comments on the improvement activities that we were planning to do. The key element of the plan was a couple of graphs, indicating the expected evolution of major quality characteristics. Today, we would call them KPIs; examples include the respective cost and percentages of scrap and rework, costs of service and warranty, etc.

I started working on it, trying to make things as realistic as possible, and taking into account the realities and limitations of the organisation. I printed everything out, and put the plan on my CEO's desk. I was rather proud of my achievement. About an hour later, he called me to his office to discuss the quality plan. This is how the discussion went...

"Thanks Willy for the plan, but you will have to change it; it will not do for the meeting."

Having put a lot of work into it, I was a bit disappointed, so I enquired, "What is wrong with it?"

"It is not that there is anything wrong with it as such, but it is not ambitious enough," he replied.

"Well, it is, in my view, the correct balance between ambitious and realistic," I added, trying to defend my work.

"I am sure it is, but I have a copy of the slides my US colleague will be presenting, and his graphs show much more ambition than yours. Here, take a look..." he went on, and he showed me the US graphs of the various quality indicators and their foreseen evolution. All non-quality cost were expected to be drastically reduced in the coming five years.

"You see, if he shows these graphs and then I show mine – well, yours – that will not make me – well, you – look good," he further explained.

From a perception point of view, that was correct and logical. However, being young and inexperienced, I still wanted to give reality a chance, so I insisted, "But there is no way the US factory will be able to achieve that kind of improvement within five years."

"No, of course not, we all know that, but you are missing the point here, Willy. None of these people on the board will remember these numbers by next year, it is irrelevant whether we achieve that target or not. The point is to look ambitious and preferably more ambitious than the other factories." As I stated in Column 5, the other factories, which are internal to the organisation, are the real competition.

Some of you may remember the British comedy series "Keeping Up Appearances." We all laughed at Hyacinth Bucket (pronounced as Bouquet), but there is a lot of self-deceit in business, as well. No better moment to experience it then when a visit from the head office is announced.

__All you asked for to make the office and the workplace look nice but were refused for cost reasons, will now be available in abundance.__

We want to show the esteemed visitors a shiny factory with workers in freshly washed overalls. In reality the factory never looks this way, but it is vital that we keep up appearances. It seems like the more important the visitors are, the more they are lied to.

Self-deceit even works on a technical level. Each time a new model was developed, every factory in the group was asked to present their production cost. The idea was to give the order to the factory with the best proposal. Again, your colleagues are your greatest competitors. Other elements were considered, like the ease of a mix with existing models, main customer locations, etc, but cost played a major part.

Product engineering drawings as well as their specifications were released, and then manufacturing engineering and purchasing started to work on the cost calculations. After much hard work, they came to a production cost and presented that to the CEO, who automatically said it was too high, and they had to do it all over again. Sometimes a couple of iterations were needed, until it was low enough for the CEO to find it acceptable.

Specifically on material specifications, I was occasionally asked for some technical assistance – as a metallurgist – but I was not really involved in the costing effort. Being a little detached from the process, I observed it in amazement.

In quality, we go by getting it *'right first time'* and *'right every time'*, so you would think that the first calculation was the good one. And if it was not, you had to fire these people because they were clearly incompetent. But these people were very competent, and their hard work was not useless or wrong. The first result they presented was correct and realistic.

When it was not accepted (as expected), they came up with a slightly tweaked price, playing their part on this stage, as so well described by Shakespeare. Purchasing would ask for price quotes with price breaks by volume. In the first calculation, they used the cost according to a realistically expected volume of the new product sales. If that was deemed too expensive, they took a price related to a higher volume, assuming, or rather pretending, that the new product would be an amazing sales success. Once you get the hang of it, it becomes easy.

In many plays written by Shakespeare, it seemed just enough living actors were left on stage to carry off the dead bodies. Our play was not that dramatic. It just always ended with the cost that the CEO had in the back of his mind from the start. That end result was sent to headquarters, and with some luck, we were given the order to produce the new model. As expected, the profit from that model was lower than foreseen, leading to the CEO being unhappy again.

> *This was the most amazing thing of the whole story: management was actually and honestly surprised about that result.*

It goes to show how strong self-deceit can be.

There are many forms of self-deceit. One is in finance, by shifting costs from one place to another and thinking you are saving money.

Many years ago, Philips underwent a severe restructuring operation, which was called *Centurion*. Note that all such plans have impressive names, but the end objective is always the same: Less Employees Are Needed (LEAN). A specialist in design of experiments and Taguchi methodologies was one of those who lost their jobs in this change. He was working with several departments on specific problems when he was relieved of his job.

That did not mean the problems he was working on had disappeared; it just meant they now lacked the knowledge to tackle them internally. Fortunately, knowledge can be hired. So, instead of doing the work as a Philips employee, he now did exactly the same thing as an independent consultant, charging them twice the amount of his former wage. In the consecutive years, he made more out of Philips than he had ever done as an employee. In addition, he noticed that as an outsider, he was better listened to by management than as an employee.

Something the Dutch solo Vice President Europe also mentioned to me. He used to work for a Swiss pharmaceutical company as a corporate quality manager. In that function, he reported directly to the CEO. Now, this was a CEO who arrived in the car park early in the morning, took the elevator to the highest floor, worked hard the whole day and left late in the evening, taking the elevator down to the car park.

He asked his quality manager what he could do for quality. One answer was to try to be more visible to the people working in the organisation, and to maybe "…get out of the elevator at a lower floor level, walk around a little and just talk to a couple of people about quality, strategy…". He did not think that was a good idea because he had absolutely no time to do so.

Years later, they met again, and the CEO was interested to hear that his former quality manager was now doing consulting work. He invited him to visit and to discuss a little bit about his current job. They had a meeting in the office on the eleventh floor, and he asked exactly the same question and received exactly the same answer. But he now replied: "*Well, maybe that is not a bad idea, I will try that.*"

Dr Deming stated that all profound knowledge must come from the outside. I disagree with this statement, because I think there is a lot of profound knowledge inside every organisation.

But outside knowledge is listened to; inside knowledge is all too often neglected.

The story above is an illustration of the fact that it is not about being right, it is about getting people to accept that you are right. Those are two different things.

One of the biggest mistakes, also often made by quality managers, is thinking that being right is enough and that everyone will recognise that and automatically agree with you. It does not work that way; communication and presentation of an idea are almost as important as the quality of the idea itself. That may sound unfair, and sometimes it actually is, but how you present things is critical. Communication skills are often lacking internally among employees; but external knowledge carriers tend to be excellent at it.

Trying to convince people to change their minds, does not work either.

The only thing you can do is to bring someone in such a state of mind that they are willing to change their own mind.

Again, the way arguments are being presented has a major impact. It requires what is known as emotional intelligence, a trendy subject some years ago, and abbreviated as EQ.

In my view, SM is a better abbreviation, and closer to the point. It stands for *Smart Manipulation*, as you obviously guessed, and it is part of your political skill set. You see, deep down there is nothing wrong with politics, it is all about the way it is used and to what purpose.

A seasoned quality manager learned me a trick on how to use an external auditor to fit your purpose.

He always compared an external auditor to a dog.

This may sound disrespectful, but the comparison comes from the similar objective of auditors and dogs: to find bones. The dogs do it to chew on them, and the auditor will do it to write a corrective action request or a non-conformance.

As a quality manager, you will have a relatively good idea of where the bones are buried. There may be some that you dug up, but being just an employee, could not get enough management attention to act on it. However, if that bone is brought to the surface by an external auditor, it is much more likely to get a response.

So, you take your auditor on a leash to the right area and suggest they dig there. The auditor will be happy to find a bone, and you are happy it is that bone. A win-win, if ever there was one.

One species of apes we did not see in Uganda is the bonobo, for the simple reason that it does not live there. They are a vulnerable species due to loss of habitat and poaching. You only find them in the Democratic Republic of the Congo, separated from the chimpanzees by the wide Congo River.

It is actually a nice example of evolution because the bonobos, although genetically very closely related to chimpanzees, developed into a different type of social animal. Bonobo communities are female-led, they are much more peaceful than chimpanzees, and solve most of their political problems with sex. Maybe we should look to them as a source of inspiration.

COLUMN 8
THE SMILE OF THE NURSE

A little patience, a kind word, a listening
ear, are more valuable to my well-being
than the medication I get.
A terminally ill patient

Modern quality management was developed in manufacturing by engineers and statisticians. Thus, it became a highly technical area with a focus on root cause analysis, statistics, and variation reduction. A whole set of quality tools was developed, and their application has brought tremendous improvements to all types of products and processes. They are still very relevant, even in today's manufacturing environment.

The importance of manufacturing, for the overall economy, however, is shrinking. One reason may be that, with thanks to quality management, products today are being made with extreme efficiency. If you analyse the price of products, including an unknown profit, it is almost beyond belief how cheap things really are.

Let me give you an example: I am a bit of a DIY (**D**[o] **I**[t] **Y**[ourself]) guy, and on a web shop, I found the Makita drill set P67832 containing 101 accessory parts for a drilling machine. It contains a spirit level, drills of different sizes for different materials, screw bits, hole saws, screwdrivers... all nicely stored in a hard plastic case. Here we have 101 parts produced by different factories, sent to a final assembly shop where they are all placed in a case (coming from yet another factory). These are then sent to a warehouse before they finally reach your doorstep. The web shop makes a profit, all producers that add to the total product make a profit, the transport company makes a profit, and you pay the total sum of €36.35 or some €0.36 per piece.

> *Next time you buy something and think it is expensive, try to make a mental map of the complete chain to get this product to you for that price. You will be amazed!*

Thus, both technological development and quality improvement have reduced all sorts of non-quality related costs. We have done a great job, and as a result, fewer jobs are required in manufacturing for an ever bigger output. Today, developed economies are service-driven, with the service sector constituting some 70% to 80% of the total economic added value.

I realised this for the first time while watching an episode of the "Inspector Morse" detective series. As usual, Detective Chief Inspector Morse, and Lewis, his down-to-earth Detective Sergeant, are investigating a murder. During the inquiry, they discovered that a so-called English brand of HiFi equipment is a Japanese product, hidden in a British-styled case.

At that point Morse asks the question: *"Why doesn't anyone make stuff anymore, Lewis?"*

"Because we live in a service economy sir," Lewis replied.

This series started in the late 1980s and ran until the mid-1990s, which indicates that we have been living in a service economy for quite some time now. Yet, quality has continued to focus on manufacturing, representing an ever smaller part of the economy. It is not that we are not trying, the point is that we do not seem to be succeeding in entering the service world. I believe this has to do with two things: the wrong language and inadequate tools.

The language problem, which I generally refer to as *lost in translation*, has to do with our background as explained above. Our success stories come from manufacturing, so when we want to introduce quality management in a hospital, we refer to Toyota and the very well-known Toyota Production System (TPS), a benchmark in quality and production.

> *This may surprise some quality experts, but nurses do not assemble cars, they care for people.*

We should not be surprised that it is hard for them to relate to that language. Even our standards (that are supposed to be universally applicable) use a language that relates much more to production than to a service environment. Not only are they very poorly written, but they also need a lot of translation to be applied in various service activities.

In the past, programmes have started in areas like healthcare and education, but not always with great success. Today, applications of Lean and Six Sigma, specifically in healthcare, tend to be more successful. We gradually learn and good examples have created more interest.

We are making progress, but mainly in back-office process based activities, very similar to production. In healthcare it involves improvement projects aimed at reducing waiting times, making sure the right medication gets to the right person, simplifying registration procedures or streamlining data. Things that can be measured and structured and organised.

> ***Make no mistake, these are very important aspects of healthcare, but they are missing one vital aspect: the impact of interactions between people.***

The same things happened often in education, where improvements were focused on organisational issues, most times leading to added administrative work for teachers. This did not make the word, *quality*, popular in education. It also did not touch on the critical aspects of educational quality: the learning process driven by the interaction between teachers and pupils or students. The tendency to apply business terms, like calling a student a client, did not help either.

In quality we are so focused on processes and technology, that we miss essential aspects of service. When I was teaching, I had my course texts copied in a local copy centre. This was a small shop with the female owner running it, occasionally helped by her daughter and husband. She also had a couple of friendly dogs walking around. Quality consultants do not often visit these very small organisations. However, VCK[3] (currently known as Xelyo), started a government-funded project to offer quality support to micro-organisations. My copy centre enlisted.

In came a seasoned quality professional, who had spent his career in large manufacturing corporations. He visited the copy centre and focused on the technical heart of the business: the copy machines. They were all of the same brand, and maintenance was performed by the producer as described in a service agreement.

As we believe we can only manage what we measure, we need data. So the consultant asked the owner to start collecting data on the machines: how many copies were taken, what printing errors occurred, how often they occurred, the number of breakdowns, how many maintenance interventions were done and so on.

She did what was asked for, but she did not see the point of it.

She was very happy with the machines and the maintenance, but had no idea how all this data-gathering work would help improve her shop

---

[3] VCK: Vlaams Centrum voor Kwaliteitszorg

and attract more customers or improve the satisfaction and loyalty of existing customers. After a couple of meetings, she called VCK and told them this was not working. The project was cancelled, but one of the ladies that worked with VCK as a project manager decided to visit the shop, to see if there was anything else she could do to help in some other way.

She entered, looked around and was greeted by the owner who approached her from the back of the shop. The project manager introduced herself and made a couple of comments: how unattractive the shop looked at first sight, that the light was not very nice, the wall colours were dull, and she even made a remark (in a polite way) about the dress and make-up of the owner.

I have been a quality management consultant for over thirty years, and I have never commented on my clients' dresses, suits or make-up. It was not really relevant to the environment I was working in. Besides, lacking knowledge of fashion and clothes, I would never notice any of these things anyway. As I have no clothing style whatsoever, perhaps my clients were thinking all sorts of things about the way I turned up. They have always been polite enough not to make any remarks, as that was not relevant to them either.

***But in an environment with
face-to-face contact between
service provider and customer,
a first impression is of the
greatest importance.***

The look, feel and general atmosphere will have a huge impact on that impression. What the customer thinks about the copy shop will be more decided by the dress of the shopkeeper than by the brand of the copy machines. No customer knows anything about that anyway.

So they sat down and looked at ways to make the shop look more attractive, working on friendliness in addressing customers, and so on. The owner ended up very happy with the outcome of the revived project. Quality is determined by how the customer feels, and in service, this is, to a large extent, related to how you are being treated by the service provider. Impressions and experiences are created on the spot as the interaction is happening.

During a trip to Iceland, we booked a guided bus tour from the little town of Kirkjubæjarklaustur (you have to love that name) to Lakagigar. The Laki Craters are very beautiful and – given good weather – you can see a range of craters formed during one of the biggest and longest volcano eruptions ever.

Sadly, we had the most appalling weather: it was cold, foggy, windy and rainy. From the top, we could see two, a maximum of three craters, far away. Yet, it was a great experience as the tour guide was an amazing man.

He told us about the history and impact of the eruption, and linked it to the French Revolution. He showed us little things to notice and appreciate, gave insights into some of the Icelandic fairy tales and got us to forget the bad weather. Well, almost.

> *These days, the internet takes care of a lot of administration in travelling, but at the end of the trip, the main factor in deciding the quality experience, will be the tour guide.*

How he or she can interact with the clients, will make all the difference.

This brings us to a second issue: inadequate tools and wrong focus. Classically in quality, we aim to reduce variation and make all products as equal as possible. We typically do that by investigating which inputs generate the biggest variation in the output. Once we know that, we try to control those inputs, by reducing their variation and/or impact. But what if the most important input is people, like a group of tourists or a class of pupils or a ward of patients?

What if variation is a given, and something to accept?

In history, there have been several attempts to eliminate human variation; it has led to some of the darkest periods in our existence. Do not try to reduce variation in people; even in the light of evolution, it is a stupid thing to do. Learn to deal with this variation because today people expect to be treated much more individually. We have not been raised like that at all; our motto was to "Treat people the way you want to be treated." This is a statement you still hear a lot today and that we keep teaching our children. It is of course a ridiculously arrogant and egocentric view on humanity.

What on earth makes you think that the eight billion other people on this planet would want to be treated the way you want to be treated?

How delusional must one be to believe that?

All that human variation and the very complex nature of human interactions, makes it much more difficult to reach the very high quality levels that we have become accustomed to in manufacturing. We talk about parts per million (ppm) defects; when referring to Six Sigma the goal is 3.4 ppm defects. In other words, if we do things one million times it may only go wrong three or four times. That is a rather unrealistic target in human interactions.

It should make us extra careful to use the term excellence. One Belgian bank captured this very well when they launched the slogan: *"We go 100% for 95% satisfied customers."* That was smart, although I am not sure everyone really understood it. The key point is that in banking, like in most services, you cannot please everyone. Investing a lot of money in trying to do so, such as aiming for 99% satisfied customers, might be a detrimental business decision.

Besides, it is the misunderstandings and the arguments that make life interesting and relations fascinating. Imagine you are on Tinder[4], and you mention in your profile that you are looking for a relationship with a maximum of 3.4 ppm errors, meaning arguments, quarrels, discussions, and the likes. Chances are very likely that you will stay single for the rest of your life. In the unlikely event

---

[4] *Tinder* is a social media dating website

that you find a nice connection on Tinder, someone who is also into Six Sigma, and looking for the same maximum 3.4 ppm defects, chances are that the two of you will be bored for the rest of your lives.

The biggest problem quality has with face-to-face services is that analysis does not work.

We are not dealing with complicated problems, but complex situations. That is an altogether different animal. For those of you who want to know more about this, google 'Cynefin'. You cannot solve a complex problem with a model based on Root Cause Analysis because each new case is different from the previous one, as you are dealing with another person. I realised this for the first time at a conference in Edmonton, Canada.

One of the speakers, from the provincial health council, talked about healthcare in remote areas, and as you know, Canada has a lot of remote areas. The improvements proposed were a myriad of actions, generally little tasks with limited to no investment, and focusing a lot on aspects of communication, understanding patients, and taking their culture and background into account.

The session manager was a seasoned quality professional, and he asked the first question: "Can you expand on what the root cause of the problem was?"

The answer was simple: "No, because there is no such thing as a root cause in these kinds of problems." As I said, it is a different animal!

We have techniques like *Five Why's* to come to what we call the *root cause*, but in reality we look for something we can act upon and then call that the root cause. Asking 'Why' five times, and thinking that gets you to the root of anything, is laughable to any four-year-old child.

If you keep asking "Why", you will realise that there is no such thing as a root cause, except maybe the Big Bang.

Are we then powerless, dependent on luck and the personality of the service provider? Not really, we can even work in a very structured way to improve the quality of face-to-face services. But we need to go about it in a different way and with different expectations.

Let me explain this with a very simple service example: a visit to the hairdresser, or perhaps more specifically, me paying a visit to a hairdresser. I already mentioned I have no clothing style whatsoever, I also do not care much about my hairdo. The main (and only) requirement being that it does not take too much time in the morning to make it look acceptable.

A quality-focused hairdresser would see this immediately as I enter his shop. That is the first thing to do: observe carefully! Think about the copy centre where observation in itself already generated several quality improvement ideas. There, it was a potential customer observing the shop and the shopkeeper, here it is the service provider observing the customer. This observation already tells him it makes no sense to propose colouring, special treatments or a complex hairdo. These proposals would just annoy me.

After welcoming me and agreeing on a very simple hairdo, the next step is, of course, cutting my hair. The assumption is that the hairdresser knows how to cut hair. We do not doubt their technical capability, but then we very rarely doubt the technical capability of the service provider.

Most patients are confident that their doctor or surgeon knows what he or she is doing.

What makes the difference in quality experience is the way the patient is treated by that competent doctor. A hairdresser, of course, will not cut into your body, unless they are really incompetent, but there are other things they can do to please or annoy you.

Talking for instance. Some people go to the hairdresser to socialise, I go when my hair has grown so long that it needs cutting or it becomes unsafe. When I enter a barber shop for the first time, the new hairdresser does not know that. The person may be a very social and talkative person and if their parents taught them to treat people the way they want to be treated, they might bore me to death with endless talking. If, on the other hand, they are aiming to treat people the way they want to be treated, they will try to find out what kind of person I am.

They can do that by asking a couple of simple, safe questions and see how I react. Am I enthusiastic, do I engage in a discussion, do I ask them questions? If so: keep talking! But if my answers are of the one word type, it might be a better idea to concentrate on cutting my hair and limiting the talk.

Here lies the clue:
you need to be genuinely
interested in understanding the
person in front of you, so you can
treat them the way they want to
be treated.

Empathy is a verb. Once that is done, the rest is easy. Well, not that easy because people are complex creatures and human interactions always have an element of unpredictability, which is why aiming for 95% satisfied customers could be a good target.

However, there is one thing that all people like: *being remembered*. When I enter the same barber shop a couple of months later, it would please me very much if the hairdresser remembers my haircut and my not very talkative nature. Being remembered gives you the feeling of being important. It does not matter whether you are or not, at least you get the feeling. And it is the person right in front of you, the front line service employee that can give you that feeling.

The example of the hairdresser is an easy one. Generally, you come out looking, and subsequently, feeling better. If the hairdresser is any good, the end result is always positive. There are many situations where it is much more difficult to obtain a good result because you simply cannot always give in to customer demands. Some things just need to be accepted by the customer.

When a customer enters a shop with a defective product and the warranty period has expired, an eventual repair will have to be paid for. That may not be to the customer's liking, but there are rules to be followed. These rules are typically set by others in the organisation who are safely behind their desks when customers complain, and who rarely even meet these customers. This makes front-end service such hard work, and that is why these people deserve much more respect than they generally get.

Just by caring for the people they serve, any service provider can improve the quality feeling they provoke within a customer without applying any quality management standard, root cause analysis or statistical methods. *A little patience, some kind words, and a lovely smile can make all the difference, even, and maybe even more so, when you are terminally ill.*

COLUMN 9
ON COMPLIANCE

Quality begins where compliance ends.
Willy Vandenbrande

When people ask me what I do for a living, and I reply that I am a quality management consultant, there are two response types that usually follow: *'ISO 9000 you mean?'* or *'What does that mean?'*

The first response typically comes from people working in commercial organisations and for whom quality has become equal to a certified ISO 9000 system. The second response comes from everybody else. Of course, that second response can be quite intimidating, because you have to think about what it is that you are really doing. It is a question that will never be asked of a teacher, a postman, a nurse or so many other professionals. The profession is the content and the contribution to society is immediately clear. What on earth does a quality management consultant contribute to? An existential question that we probably all should ask ourselves from time to time, regardless of our job.

In Column 5, I mentioned that in 1990 I attended the 3½-day seminar that Dr W E Deming delivered in Birmingham, United Kingdom. The date is important in relation to ISO 9000, because that set of international standards on quality management systems was released at the end of 1987. It created a lot of buzz, and the early 1990s saw an exponential increase in the attention to, and certification of, quality management systems that comply to the relevant ISO 9000 standard.

In the Deming seminar at the end of each day, people were invited to ask questions. One of the attendees asked Dr Deming what he thought about this standard and the accompanying certification process. He replied that it could be a start, an interesting first step, but certainly never a replacement for Total Quality Management.

At dinner later that day, one of the people at my table came back to this answer and made a comment in the following words:

"This just shows how he (Dr Deming) is totally out of touch with the current world of quality. Just have the system certified and get it over with."

In other words, once we comply to the Standard and have a compliance maintenance system in place, we have fulfilled our quality job. A limited and simplified view on quality to say the least!

But people like simplicity and so do companies. So, in large parts of the industry the simple solution to supplier quality became: *'Get certified!'* As this line of thinking spread very quickly, in no time, everyone had to be certified, so they got the certificate. Well, congratulations to you, but of course also to all your competitors. They have all obtained their ISO 9000 certificate. That should have made it clear to everyone that the certificate could never be the end of quality, but merely a start.

Apart from quality certifications, there are several other requirements that you have to fulfil in order to be allowed in specific markets. Legal requirements, sector specific rules, customer specific demands, the list is long and getting longer. Fulfilling all these requirements has been translated into one simple term: *compliance*.

Compliance allows you to participate, but it does not guarantee you a win. I often compare it with the Olympic Games where there are qualification criteria to be allowed to enter the competition. Reaching these, and participating, is a great achievement, but it does not automatically win you a medal.

In fact, the one thing that in no way distinguishes you from your competitor, is compliance.

They are all compliant, otherwise they would not be your competitors. Surprisingly, this very logical and evident conclusion is not always seen as such. Many quality departments have as their most important, and sometimes only task, to manage the system and ensure the organisation passes the certification audits. You need to fulfil customer requirements, so if a customer demands it, you have to do it as one of your tasks, but never as your only task.

In hindsight, I wonder whether the ISO 9000 series of standards were a good thing for quality. In the 1980s, quality management was very prominent, with conferences drawing large crowds, and our gurus like Deming and Juran were very popular.

To a large extent, this had to do with the industrial success of Japan and the observation that quality was not a cost but a profit centre. Maybe more correctly, it should be seen as an investment that gives a return in the form of increased market share and profitability due to avoided non-quality related costs. Quality managers were important and present at the strategic level of organisations. And then came ISO 9000.

President Truman criticised his economic advisors because they would always say, '...on the one hand, so-and-so, but on the other hand, an entirely opposite so-and-so!'

It made him call out for one-handed advisors.

I am afraid I would not qualify as a good advisor for him, because in reality, many cases just have two sides to them. As Johan Cruijff, the famous Dutch football player, expressed it, *"Every advantage has its disadvantage."*

On the one hand, ISO 9000 created awareness for the need for a good quality management system. Specifically for smaller organisations, it offered a structured and standardised way to build a strong foundation for quality. On the other hand, for many people, it reduced quality to complying to a standard and quality management to a separate task for specialists of standards. These are two thoughts that made true total quality management more difficult.

There does not have to be a contradiction between compliance and total quality. A good system can be the perfect foundation for total quality management, but that is definitely not always the case.

The goal is all too often to obtain the certificate with minimal effort and cost, and not to start a total quality management process.

ISO 9000 certification started a successful business of quality. I sometimes wonder if we are not more concerned about the business of quality than about the quality of business. I can testify (*perhaps confess*) to this, as it has been a major source of income for me as well for several years.

Working for a small consulting agency in the early 1990s, most of my work was to help companies build a system that could be certified. When I started my own business, I gradually shifted my work to process improvement. That was more fun, it was less predictable, and more satisfying for the engineer and amateur statistician in me.

I kept on supporting some of my ISO 9001 clients with internal auditing and adaptations with each new version of the standard. These new versions have proven to be a real cash cow for the business of quality, starting with the International Organisation for Standardisation itself, and then followed by consulting and certification. The standard has evolved from a contractual agreement between the customer and the supplier (1987 and 1994 versions) to a model based on process thinking (2000 and 2008 versions) and to end – until the next change – by adding risk-based thinking to it (2015 version).

Companies have proven to be extremely flexible because within three years after the release of the 2000 version, as good as all of them became process-based, and as of 2018, they were all committed to risk-based thinking. Well, this is what I presume, as hardly any of them lost their certificate along the way.

One thing is constant over all the versions: they are all written in a horrible language.

I wanted to write *in horrible English*, but that would be such an insult to the beautiful English language. But then, it is badly written in all languages, so it is an insult to all of them. People who are knowledgeable about these standards will probably point out my sloppy use of the term ISO 9000. In fact, the certifiable norm, the one that contains the actual requirements, is the ISO 9001 standard.

Checking with our National Standards Bureau, the ISO 9001:2015 standard today costs €142.00 (one hundred and forty-two euros). This is actually a rather expensive book, considering the limited number of pages.

The 2015 EOQ Congress (European Organisation for Quality) in Athens was, to a large extent, devoted to the 2015 version of the standard to be released later that year. In one of the sessions, a contributor to TC 176, which is the Technical Committee responsible for the development of quality management standards, explained the major changes that were included.

Some of the participants were rather critical and specifically had problems with the vagueness of the term, *risk-based thinking*. The speaker replied that it was very important to hire someone with good knowledge of the standards to help you translate the text for your situation. In other words: get yourself a good and experienced consultant, because this is highly specialised material.

I found that to be quite a remarkable answer. Many people have described ISO 9001 as *common business sense*, which is logical and correct as it is basically a text on quality management with requirements that should be understandable for all.

Apparently, it has been written in such a way, that most people need a specialist to understand common business sense.

Imagine you go to a bookshop and you select a book that costs a whopping €140.00. Then, at the check-out counter, the shopkeeper tells you that in order to understand it, you will need to hire someone at €1,000.00 per day to read and interpret it for you. Would you buy that book?

Fortunately, there are people out there to help you in a much cheaper way. There is a book for sale for some €10.00 that promises to explain ISO 9001:2015 in *plain English*. Clearly, the author feels the original is written in *un-plain* English! If you ever wondered what that looks like, read ISO 9001. Standards' organisations are making a fortune out of this Standard, so the least they could do is to make it readable.

Apart from the language issue, there is a second and even more important reason why I am critical of the Standard.

If you want to make sure a CEO loses all interest in quality, tell them to read the ISO 9001 Standard.

Success guaranteed. As I have indicated, this really is the most distributed text on quality management, and no one I have ever known anywhere in the entire world, has become enthusiastic about quality by reading it.

Imagine you are on a first date in a nice restaurant and all seems to be going well. As you want to keep the conversation going, you ask your date what she does for a living, and she says she is a teacher at the local primary school.

Then she asks you: *'And what do you do for a living?'* And you proudly reply: *'I am the quality manager of company XYZ.'*

She looks at you and repeats, *'So, what is it that you do then?'* as very few people have a clue of what a quality manager does all day.

So you start to explain as best you can, but you notice that the more you say, the less interested she looks. You start to panic because she is really nice, and you do not want to spoil the moment. All of a sudden, you realise that you have the key to her heart – and maybe some other body parts – with you. It is with great relief that you say: I have here a copy of the ISO 9001 Standard, and this is the document that describes the essence of what I am doing. Take it with you, and when you find the time, read it. Then, we can discuss it on our next date.

If you are unlucky and she does find the time to read it, the chances of that second date will probably have come down drastically.

I used this analogy with a group of young quality professionals, and one of the participants fully agreed. Not just about the Standard, but even about mentioning the profession of a quality manager. *'Next time, I will say that I am a pilot,'* was the conclusion he had drawn out of his failed attempts at dating. He clearly presumed pilots were seen as sexier than quality managers; how come?

Apart from our obsession with non-quality, the focus on compliance is another reason why quality management is not very popular. Phil Crosby found an analogy between quality and sex: it is a natural human habit, everybody wants it and everyone thinks he is an expert. The last sentence makes the joke, but it is also a bit spiteful as Crosby found himself an expert (in quality, I mean) and rightly so, but so are most customers. People know whether or not they have been treated in a quality way.

The most important sentences are the first two. It is a natural human habit, is quite clear as our cultural development is completely directed towards creating a better life, if not for us, at least for our children. And yes, everybody wants a good quality life, but most still do not like quality management. This is especially so if it is all about rules, regulations, instructions and paperwork that is not seen to add any value. It can become a system that prevents people from doing a good job rather than supporting them. Actually, some legal requirements or sectoral requirements are sometimes more responsible for this than ISO 9001 requirements, but it all adds up.

Some years ago, I had a rather serious shoulder injury, and my doctor referred me to a specialist to evaluate if surgery might be necessary. The surgeon was a very friendly guy, and to obtain a diagnosis, he got me to do some exercises, watched an X-ray, and then asked me what I did for a living.

I told him I was a quality management consultant. That completely changed the atmosphere.

The hospital he was working in was going through a quality programme, and the process drove him totally mad. Rules were introduced that made no sense to him and his colleagues, but that did increase the administrative burden. His biggest concern was that this administration was taking away time he could devote to his patients.

There is also serious doubt about the way quality is evaluated. My wife worked her entire professional life in education. Towards the end of her career, schools underwent visitations aimed at evaluating the quality of the educational institution. We would call it an audit. It was always a frustrating exercise, and with one complaint from all involved: *'The only thing that matters is that everything looks good on paper.'*

You could say this simply means the audits were no good, but the more rules there are, the more the time needed to check if the rules were followed. That leaves less time to evaluate the effectiveness and value of the rules. And even worse: there is less time to focus on what really matters, the *teaching process*.

Note that this is no better in companies. During a discussion with quality managers on training and qualification, one of the participants explained the system they had as follows: *'For each job, we have a description of the skills needed to do that job, people are trained and qualified, and we keep records of all those who are qualified.'* Someone then asked if it was always possible to stick to that list, and the answer was:

'Well, sometimes we do have problems when people fall ill or are on holiday, but on the days of the audit, only qualified people perform the jobs.'

On audit days, it all looks good.

The problem is that this obsession with certificates is becoming visible in sustainability. The current state of the planet is, to say the least, not very good. Although there is a lot of talk about the subject, the actual results are not (yet?) showing.

Global warming is a good example. The IPCC (Intergovernmental Panel on Climate Change) has existed since 1988, as well as the associated international meetings (COP – Conference of the Parties) have been held every year since 1995. For almost thirty years now, the only observation that can be made is a steady increase of CO_2 content in the atmosphere. There are lots of words and historic moments (Kyoto 1997, Paris 2015) but not enough actions to show positive results.

Several systems exist to help you improve your organisation's impact on sustainability. These systems typically lay a high emphasis on reporting (to measure is to know), and some kind of certification scheme is generally part of the system. One example of is the B-Corps system, which is enjoying a growing popularity in Europe.

I once attended an online session of the European branch of B-Corps with an introduction to the system and a couple of presentations by companies that held the certificate. All of the presenters emphasised that sustainability was the key issue to look for and not the certificate. While they were saying this, questions came in through the chat. *'How long does it take to get certified?' 'What is the cost of the certificate?' 'What is the value of the certificate in my market?'*

> **In short, 95% of the questions were about the certificate, the remaining 5% about the impact on sustainability.**

Recently, in an interest group discussing quality and sustainability, one of the participants worked for a company that was B-Corps certified. She had actually been the person most involved in setting up the system. The group moderator asked her if she was happy with the result and would do it again, but she was hesitant to answer positively on both questions.

Not that there was anything wrong with the system they implemented, but there are plenty of them around, so was B-Corps the best choice? There was also the added comment that improvement of the situation is determined by the commitment of the organisation to do something about it, regardless of the system used.

She referred to the Corporate Sustainability Reporting Directive (CSRD), issued by the European Union and made it clear that the organisation would not keep two reporting systems on sustainability, especially not if one is to be a legal requirement. Note that the directive talks about reporting. Knowing where you are is a good start for improvement, but resources are limited. Spending a lot on measuring and reporting will mean less is available for action. The European Commission missed an opportunity, in my view; they should have called it CSRID, Corporate Sustainability Reporting and Improvement Directive.

We all know analysis paralysis[5], but there is also something called measurement paralysis. The idea behind it is that, *because we do not know exactly what the situation is, we cannot take any action*.

In quality, we know there is no such thing as a true value; there is an operational definition linked to a measurement system, which leads to a valid result, within the limits of the operational definition. Hence, measuring according to this definition will allow us to see the evolutions in the results, as well as the consequences of our actions.

> ***One way of stalling action is to come up with another operational definition, claim it is more accurate or relevant, and start measuring all over again.***

As I already mentioned, in Belgium, like in many other countries, we have serious problems with traffic jams. Some five or six years ago, the then minister of traffic announced a new measurement system that would accurately show the position and length of traffic jams. This new system would give us much better information about the traffic

---

[5] *Analysis paralysis* is term used to say analyses have been overly carried out on something till it loses its value

problem and allow us to take more focused actions.

Now, if aliens were to land in Belgium and listen to the radio news for one week, they would know where the traffic jams are. In fact, anyone in Belgium knew, and knows where the traffic jams are. Today, they are more or less in the same places as ten years ago, and none of them have become shorter. Luckily, thanks to our new and accurate measurement system, we now know exactly how long they are: quite an achievement, but of little comfort to the people in the queue. It is vital that we measure things, but if these measurements do not lead to action, we will simply observe that the situation is getting worse.

Being compliant is important. You cannot avoid it, but you should make sure that you create a system on which action for improvement can be built. Do not let that opportunity go to waste!

COLUMN 10
BUSINESS ETHICS

And what is good, Phaedrus, and what is
not good – Need we ask anyone to tell
us these things.

Robert M Pirsig

In the early 1990s, not long after the fall of
the Berlin Wall, and the start of the
democratisation of Eastern Europe, I was
one of three speakers in a conference/training
course in Budapest, Hungary.

Each of us gave several presentations that
filled a two-day programme. In addition, we
visited a couple of companies. The event was
organised by VCK and the Hungarian Society
for Quality, and I believe there was financial
support from the European Union. I have very
good memories of that conference because of
the warm welcome I received, the attentive
and interested audience, and the city's beauty.

Not all the participants understood English,
so translation was foreseen by a retired
professor of English literature. He was such a
kind man, and he had the challenging task of
doing all translations for all the speakers. We

had some rest in between lectures, but he had to work continuously and did an absolutely awesome job with his on-the-spot translation.

I would make a statement in English, which he subsequently translated into Hungarian. I could then go on with the next sentence. That had a direct impact on the duration of a presentation and we had to take it into account in the timing of our speeches.

Some of the people did understand English, and that made it a special experience. I would tell a joke in English, and half of the audience laughed, then he translated it into Hungarian, and the other half laughed. As timing is vital in comedy, it did not always work out well, but it was fun to do.

One of my colleagues gave an overview of the evolution of quality management. He pictured the steps from product-oriented quality to process control, and further expanded into companywide quality, including the entire supply chain. He then made a little prediction, noting that business ethics could be next. He illustrated it using the term '*no mafia business.*' In hindsight, one could say that we underestimated the importance of the impact on society at that time. This later translated into social responsibility, and today, in sustainable development as reflected in the 17

United Nations Sustainable Development Goals (UN SDGs).

The Pirsig quote in the subtitle states that the difference between good and bad is such that it does not require explanation from anyone else. By the way, if you ever want to read a good book on quality, read "Zen and the Art of Motorcycle Maintenance" by Robert M Pirsig.

> *When talking about social responsibility and ethics, I often refer to the CEO as the Chief Ethics Officer.*

You would think he does not have to ask anyone else what it means to behave ethically. Nevertheless, there are standards available for companies to understand what is good and what is not good. Not that these standards prevent unethical behaviour, but at least they give a guideline. Are people in quality management, by nature, more inclined to behave ethically? I am afraid I will have to disappoint you; it is personal, and about how you behave, regardless of your functional role.

In 1992, the European Organization for Quality (EOQ) Congress was held in Brussels. It had close to one thousand participants; something modern-day EOQ congresses can only dream of. Amongst other sessions, a roundtable one was planned on Statistical Process Control (SPC). One of panellists had to excuse himself a couple of days before the event, and the organisers asked me to replace him. I gladly accepted the invitation.

At that time, one of the Belgian business magazines organised a *Quality Manager of the Year* award. I was not happy with it, and wrote to the editor to express my view that it was not a wise thing to do. It gives the impression that quality is obtained through an exceptional quality manager, rather than through a quality culture supported by all, and driven by the company leadership. I never got a reply to my comment.

Funny enough, the selected *Quality Manager of the Year* for that year was one of the panellists. He had won the contest on the strength of a very beautiful presentation on the quality strategy of his company, that he had helped to develop. It was revolutionary as he paid major attention on social responsibility, and with extra focus on protecting the environment. It promoted quality as a means of sustainability before that word was mainstream in business. He saw the future better than we did at that time.

The session went as follows: a couple of case studies on the use of SPC were presented, then there was a break, and afterwards, the panel discussion was held. During the break, I had coffee and a casual conversation with the *Quality Manager of the Year* awardee. He was very optimistic about the congress, and particularly pleased with the high number of participants.

Again, in hindsight, he was right! Today, getting one thousand people to attend an EOQ conference is almost impossible. But I had gone through the list of participants and made a comment to him that I often make at quality conferences:

> **Yes, there is quite a crowd, but most of them are actually active in quality. We are very good at convincing the already convinced. We preach for a flock of already converted followers.**
> **What is missing here is participants from other departments and specifically from upper management, like plant managers, CEOs etc.**

He just nodded, and at that time, the break was over and we went back on stage.

The moderator introduced the *Quality Manager of the Year* first, and asked him to give his views and comments. He stood up, went to the microphone and said: "*I think this is a great conference, but where are the plant managers, where are the CEOs, where are the business leaders? They are the ones that should be here to learn about quality, and to drive it in their organisations. All too often, we are convincing the already convinced.*"

He received a deserved standing ovation for his extremely wise words.

Note that he did not say something like *...as I was talking to my colleague during the break* or anything else along these lines for that matter. He implied he had invented all of this on the spot, something you would expect, of course, from a *Quality Manager of the Year*. I sat, watched and listened in amazement. I had prepared a couple of comments regarding SPC, and some additions to what the speakers had said, bringing that forward in the debate.

That afternoon, I learned that even when people talk about business ethics, and have the most beautiful slides, it does not mean they behave ethically. The same goes for companies with missions and values about honesty, respect and care for the environment, but we still had Dieselgate and Enron, and many other scandals.

Maybe I am just being oversensitive, calling certain business behaviours, unethical, which others do not see as such. Do not ever assume everybody thinks the way you think.

During a seminar on applying digital technology, specifically on the use of Artificial Intelligence (AI), I had a conversation with two ladies who worked for an editorial company. They specialised in professional publications, mainly directed at law firms. They already applied the powers of digitisation in their operating processes for productivity increase and cost savings, but they were also looking for new business models based on AI.

One of their ideas was to gather all information about all trials on business-related issues. Then, we offer law firms the option to subscribe to our AI system, which will give them information on what arguments a particular judge tends to be sensitive to on specific topics. That would give these law firms (and their clients) a competitive advantage when entering a lawsuit on that topic with that judge. They were looking for contacts with companies that could help them develop a system doing exactly that.

I could understand the business logic of such a system but commented on the morality of it. *"One party in a trial, able to afford this AI-based system, would have a serious advantage over the other parties involved. Does that not endanger fair justice?"*

In my entire life, I have never been stared at so intensely and in such total amazement. It was not that they were thinking about how to respond to me, they simply could not even begin to understand my doubts regarding ethics and fairness in justice. Only an utterly naïve idiot could come up with a comment like that. To them the very essence of any lawsuit was to win it.

Who on earth would care about fair justice in a court of law?

With our to-be-developed AI product, our customers will increase their chances of winning court cases, and subsequently, they will be willing to pay large sums of money to us. We are talking business models here.

It goes to show that we live in a society dominated by economic values. In reference to the interpretation of the Declaration of Independence, the pursuit of happiness seems to have been replaced by the pursuit of money, as if the two would be the same. Plenty of research show that above a certain level, more money does not make people happier, but still, we seem to be driven to gather more for the sake of gathering and having it. An added motivation could be that if you have a really big amount of money, power comes with it.

In presentations, I sometimes ask people to shut their eyes and think about the happiest moments in their respective lives. I then ask if they were buying something at that moment. Besides the occasional engineer remembering when he bought his iPad 4, most people were thinking about something else. A birth, a marriage, an encounter... something relating to a feeling-filled interaction with others.

Ethics is a part of human civilisation; it does not occur in nature.

But of all the systems we have created, our economic system is the least civilised.

It creates a world of winners and losers; let us be honest, we all prefer to be winners, and there is little mercy for losers. Abba[6] sang about it a long time ago: *'The winner takes it all,'* regardless of consequences. The editorial AI system is a good example of this.

---

[6] Abba is a Swedish pop band formed in Stockholm in 1972

Not being civilised does not mean, not being successful. *Au contraire*, our economic system has proven to be extremely successful. The same may be true about people: being egocentric often helps one succeed. Maybe there is no such thing as business ethics, or putting it differently, being ethical in business could be a barrier to maximising profits.

In a BBC documentary on ultra-processed foods, Dr Chris van Tulleken ate a diet packed with processed foods during one month. It made him feel ten years older and he was seven kilogrammes heavier. The programme was about the link between ultra-processed foods and the obesity epidemic of children. The title of the documentary was *"What are we feeding our kids?"*

He interviewed a representative of the food industry and asked if profit was more important than the health of children.

The immediate reply was that profit is always the most important thing for any company. He then went on to explain that there has been no (or at least, not enough) scientific proof that ultra-processed foods were unhealthy, and contributed to obesity. It is the reverse precautionary principle; if not proven to be bad, it is presumed to be good. A principle that has been applied for decades, and very effectively, by the tobacco and oil industries.

For a while, I participated in a group of management consultants and academics discussing the 17 UN SDGs. To me, the contribution of business to sustainability, as expressed by the SDGs, would require more ethical business behaviour. I referred to the statement that profit was always the most important for a company, even beyond children's health, as an example of what a sustainable business should not be. To my surprise, within this group of people concerned about sustainability, I was on my own with my view. As I have already indicated, never assume others think like you.

In fact, in one of the later meetings, a member of that discussion group raised the question, *"This is all very nice, but how are we going to make money out of this?"* All this sustainability talk is nice, but if it does not bring us any money, what's the point? I hate to admit it, but he probably expressed a view shared by many.

We will save ecosystems, if saving them brings more money than destroying them.

For a food company to grow and increase profits, they need more people eating more. I once heard a doctor say that if the food industry required cocaine to make people addicted to food, they would add it. Of course, they get the same result with sugar, which is legal and much cheaper.

As the saying goes, anything good in life is either illegal, immoral or fattening; it is clear that the food industry serves the last one well. People eat more, and obesity is becoming a bigger problem than hunger. This then leads to a very successful diet and slimming medication industry. You cannot say it does not work!

Recently, during a session with several textile and fashion companies on the subject of sustainability and due diligence, the topic of a *liveable wage* came up. One of the companies was positively mentioned for working with their suppliers to try to come to a liveable wage for the mainly female workers who sewed their clothes. This was seen as special achievement, or at least, a noticeable effort at being socially responsible. Apparently, the standard practice is that to make a liveable wage, these women have to work many extra hours beyond a normal schedule.

One of the things that is often looked at in making overall production more efficient is eliminating, or at least, reducing, so-called non-value-adding activities. It is a well-known technique in quality management to create a value stream map to see where productivity improvements can be made. One of the classical non-value-adding activities is called *transport*, the movement of products. Nothing has been changed to the product between the start and the end position, so its value is the same. However, this is not the way our modern economy works.

Subcontractors produce clothes very cheaply, and quite often in the Far East. By just shipping them to a shop in Western Europe, the price of the product increases by a factor of three or four, at least.

> ***In the entire process, nothing adds more value to that product than transporting it, so never let anyone tell you that transport is non-value-added.***

It is estimated (Clean Clothes Campaign) that factory workers will receive, at best, 3% of the shop selling price. Under those conditions, women have to work very hard, sewing luxury clothing, and if they are lucky – working for a socially responsible clothing brand – they will receive an *almost* liveable wage.

Imagine it is seen as unacceptable and unethical that someone works a full schedule and does not earn a liveable wage. In that dream world, the wages of the people actually making the clothes could easily be about double of what they are today, giving them a liveable life. As transport is the price-determining factor, hardly anyone further down the chain would really notice. But profit would not be maximised, and today, that is clearly seen as highly unethical.

Survival of the fittest is often used as the guiding principle of economics, presenting it as a natural thing to do in a competitive environment. It only shows that people have no knowledge of evolution, and the true meaning of survival of the fittest. The mistake is mixing biological evolution with human or cultural evolution. It so often happens, maybe because the difference is just a subtle small word.

> ### *Biological evolution is about adapting to nature, cultural evolution is about adapting nature.*

With the added observation that biological evolution is a random process and cultural evolution a driven one, and that *adapting nature*, to a large extent, has been a euphemism for destroying nature.

In 1987, the UN Brundtland Commission defined sustainable development as a balance of economic, social and environmental development. The definition is repeatedly referred to when sustainability is cited.

Today, it is often stated, that too much attention goes to the environment (the planet P) at the expense of the economy (the profit or prosperity P). Sometimes this is even referred to, in a less subtle way, as *'green madness'*. Thanks to the UN SDGs it is fairly simple to check the validity of this statement. You would think that economists, being obsessed with data, would have long done so.

Let me help them a little by looking at the evolution of the UN SDGs since their start in 2015. The latest available data was published in 2023, and refers to the 2022 measurement data. It shows a very slow evolution overall. The idea of reaching any target by 2030, is laughable if it was not that sad.

The world has not become a safer place; the Peace Index has actually dropped by 1.6%, with the Ukraine war[7] playing an important

---

[7] Russia invaded Ukraine on February 22, 2022, which resulted in a war which is still ongoing as at the time of publication

part in that. If you look at the progress made overall, and divide that over the remaining four Ps (People, Planet, Prosperity and Partnership), a pattern emerges.

Of the improvement made, 42% is attributed to Prosperity, 25% to People, 25% to partnerships, and a mere 8% to Planet. So, according to the stated data, sustainable development is pretty much about everything, except the state of the biosphere.

Even more spectacular: the only SDG that has drastically improved is SDG 9 on Industry, Innovation and Infrastructure, the major driver of economic growth. It increased by 15.8% between 2015 and 2022. Over the same time, the Planet SDGs increased by only 1.05%.

In other words, the state of the planet grew fifteen times slower than the investment in economic growth.

I hope these data can set economists at ease, as there is clearly no need to become depressed for a lack of attention to prosperity.

The UN SDGs are just one way of measuring sustainable development and the state of the planet. Another way of expressing the latter is Earth Overshoot Day. This calculates the date when people have consumed what the planet can deliver in one year. As a simple example, suppose we have a small forest of one hundred trees that can produce a wood biomass equivalent of one tree a year. If we cut (consume) two trees, the overshoot day for that forest would be June 30 because after half a year we would have consumed all that the forest can produce. Also note that the following year, the forest can only produce 0.99 tree equivalent biomass. The actual calculation is much more complicated, but this gives you an idea of how it works.

Beyond the overshoot date, we start consuming Earth's reserves. Like the SDGs, the Earth Overshoot Day also shows results by country. This calculates the overshoot date if the world population were to live (and consume) like the people in that specific country do. Comparing the two leads to remarkable results.

According to the 2022 numbers, Finland is Earth's most sustainably developed country. Overall, it scored 86.8 on a scale of 100. That is truly exceptional, and close to excellent, and we should congratulate the Fins for this result.

Finland's Earth Overshoot day for 2022 has been calculated to be March 31.

So, if the entire world population was to live like the Fins, the most sustainably living people on Earth, we would need four (4) planets to keep on fulfilling our consumption needs.

The last time I counted, there was only one. Being balanced and believing that sustainable development is not the environment and the planet alone, seems to be quite a highly unsustainable concept for that planet, and subsequently, for us. In hindsight, one could say that the UN Brundtland Commission in 1987 convicted Earth's biosphere to death by a thousand cuts.

Another measure for the state of the biosphere is the Planetary Boundaries, as defined by the Stockholm Resilience Centre. They just published the 2023 state of the planet. It shows that of the nine defined boundaries, six have been crossed. Imagine you have produced two containers of a product with nine critical dimensions on the drawing. During quality control, we discover that six of these dimensions are out of specification (out-of-spec). As the responsible quality manager, would you send those parts to the customer? And if yes, would you sleep well at night?

Maybe we need to explore space, and find other liveable planets, but we should never forget that we are in space on a (so far) liveable planet. It has been correctly described as Spaceship Earth. What would Captain Kirk do if Lieutenant Uhura told him that, out of the nine critical technical systems of the USS Enterprise, six were malfunctioning? Take it to warp speed or start an intensive maintenance programme?

There used to be a radio programme in Belgium titled *"The situation is hopeless, but not serious."* I do not think the situation is hopeless yet, but if we continue to treat it as not serious, it might become hopeless.

Our major problem is our inability to grasp the timescales. We discuss long-term strategy, and look five years ahead. We simply lack the imagination to look generations ahead, so we can consider the consequences of a model that needs more people to consume more. We think that what has brought us here, our so far successful economic growth model, will keep getting us further. This is despite the fact of evidence for the opposite staring us in the face.

West Flanders is a province in Belgium where about 1.2 million people live, myself included. It is an economically very successful region, and very much in need of additional workforce. Like most developed countries, we have an ageing population (also myself included), so it is difficult to find enough employees locally. One idea recently launched is to look for workers from India and Mexico with an estimated fifty thousand people needed by 2030. This is deemed absolutely necessary *if we want to keep our prosperity*, in other words, if we want to stay rich.

Suppose we find enough people from these places who are willing to come and work for us, that would significantly increase the province's population, even without considering some of them with a partner and/or children. All these people will obviously need housing; their children (brought to, or made in Belgium) will need to go to school, when they are ill, they will need to have access to healthcare, etc.

That is a huge task in itself, because today, there is not only a shortage of people for the industry; there is also a housing crisis, a lack of practitioners in healthcare and a severe shortage of teachers. The latter is often – and in my view, rightly so – indicated as a reason for the decline in educational quality. It is clearly a serious challenge.

Now, let us add long-term, generational thinking to the challenge and see what happens.

So far in this entire discussion, I have heard no one mention that people from India and Mexico age too.

Unfortunately for them, they are not forever young. So, at some point in time, and not that far ahead, more people will be needed. Partly to take care of them and partly to keep the economy continuously growing.

Older people not only need more care, but have also learned that consuming more is not the most valuable thing in life. Playing with and caring for their grandchildren for free is much more fun. But unpaid work is not work so they are a bit of a nuisance: no longer productive, and not buying much either.

Never before in history have so many people been at work in Belgium as today, and yet our biggest problem seems to be that not enough people are working. This is why we need to import them from elsewhere. At the same time, political parties that rally against immigration are very successful everywhere in the rich world, and it is the same in Belgium. This is the *catch-22* we have reached: *to keep growing, we need more people we do not want*. People in India and Mexico had better think twice before coming over.

Elon Musk has nine, ten or eleven children (the last I read) because he knows that if he is to sell ever more Tesla vehicles, there needs to be more people buying them, and he gives the good example for all to follow. Sustainability is not an issue; there are plenty of planets to migrate to. In that utopia, not even the sky is the limit.

In the real world, Earth's biosphere is the limit, and we are crossing its boundaries ever faster. By focusing on growth, we are selling the wrong dream, which might be the most unethical thing to do.

COLUMN 10½
CHRONICLE OF A DEATH
FORETOLD

> My proposal is to abolish the
> department of general affairs.
> **Leona Cassiani**

And so we have arrived at the 10½th Column of this book, the final Column. In the Barnes novel, this is a description of heaven. There are many ways of imagining heaven. David Byrne and Talking Heads saw it as a place where nothing ever happens. On the other hand, Julian Barnes describes it as a place where everything you can imagine happens and with unbelievable success.

Whatever you do or touch turns into gold, and you are truly awesome at everything you do, your ultimate LinkedIn ambition (*I am not here to be average, I am here to be awesome* – see Column 2) is finally realised. The most gorgeous partners fall for your charms, you play soccer and win the world cup, pick up tennis and win Wimbledon, start playing golf and win the Masters. You know what they say about ball sports: the smaller the ball, the more arrogant the players, but even when playing golf you are charming, witty and liked by all. You achieve perfection in everything you do, and this goes on into eternity.

Well, not really, because having the most awesome life with nothing but success, turns out to be hopelessly boring. It is excellence leading to death by boredom and killed by perfection. In the end, the book's main character has only one remaining wish for the masters of the universe: "*Please let me enter this place where nothing, nothing ever happens.*" He realises David Byrne was right and that endless peace and quiet is the only true heavenly state, where one is saved by death.

> **In any event, whether heaven is a place where everything is perfect, or where nothing ever happens, it will be a place where quality management is not needed.**

We live by the grace of imperfections and the presence of problems, and the more the better, from a job security point of view. So, if we ever reach our illustrious target of excellence and perfection, or nothing happens so nothing can go wrong, we will be useless forever and ever.

This may sound a little strange, but for anyone in quality management, the only final and ultimate objective must be to make themselves, or rather their job, redundant. Suppose everyone in the organisation does their job to perfection with quality embedded in everything being done. In that case, we have reached a total quality culture and no longer need quality management staff. I have given several presentations on the future of quality, explaining that Total Quality will be achieved when quality management, as a function, is no longer needed.

I would strongly advise you to read a book that contains a similar statement, but is infinitely more beautifully written, titled: '*El Amor En Los Tiempos Del Cólera,*' or '*Love in Times of Cholera*' in English, by Gabriel García Márquez. Leona Cassiani mentioned in the subtitle is a character from that book. The title of this Column was also inspired by Márquez, as the attentive reader has obviously already noticed.

For those who have not read *Love In Times Of Cholera* (you really should!), I will give a very short summary, up to the point of its interest for us here.

As a teenager, Florentino Ariza falls in love with the beautiful Fermina Daza, only to see her marry another socially and financially more suitable man. As a result, he is devastated, and emotionally incapable of loving and engaging with anyone anymore.

He does have 622 lovers in the ensuing fifty years, but no one to love. One of the people he meets is a sex worker called Leona Cassiani. She asks Florentino if he could help her get a different job; so, he introduces her to Uncle Léon XII, the owner of the river ferry company he works for as operations manager. She ends up getting the lowest paid job, in the Department of General Affairs.

What happens in the Department of General Affairs is rather vague and unclear, even to Uncle Léon XII himself. He decides to do what a quality manager would do: "I will do *an audit so I see for myself what is going on there and how this department can be made more efficient.*"

He talks with pretty much everyone, returns to his office and realises that he has ended up with more questions than answers. That happens sometimes with audits. The only one who did not speak up during the audit was the lowest-ranked employee, Leona Cassiani. She does have an opinion, and she writes a little memo for Florentino and asks him, begs him, to show it to Uncle Léon XII.

The note is of surprising simplicity. Florentino and Uncle Léon XII were thinking about having a thorough department restructuring, but Leona thinks in a totally different direction. In her opinion, there is no need for a Department of General Affairs. Her brief audit report says:

"The Department of General Affairs is a trashcan for annoying problems that other departments want to get rid of. The solution is, consequently, to abolish the Department of General Affairs, and to send the problems back to where they came from, and to tell the other departments to clean up their own mess."

It is amazing how one can say so much in just two sentences. The first sentence is a description that will sound familiar if you are working in quality, and the second is like the best description ever of true total quality: everyone cleans up their own mess!

Her proposal is executed, and Leona is promoted as assistant to Florentino, and becomes the right hand of Uncle Léon XII. Basically, she runs the entire organisation, keeping the men above her happy by making them think they are important and needed.

Is the quality world working in the direction of making itself redundant? I sometimes think we do, and sometimes we do not, but in both cases, we often do things in the wrong way or for the wrong reasons. We should be doing it structured and planned, so that quality thrives with an ever-smaller quality department.

Let me illustrate how not to do it by confessing a mistake I made many years ago. I was the quality manager, and one of the tasks of the quality department was to organise patrol inspection. An inspector walks through the plant, and randomly picks a container with parts marked as released for the next operation. These parts should be within specification, but to check the quality of our self-control system, the patrol inspector randomly measures a couple of parts. If all went well, he should never find bad parts, but of course, things do not always all go well.

We regularly needed new inspectors, and looked for them within the current machine operators: people that know the parts, processes, and machines. An inspector was better paid than an operator, and inspectors mostly worked in an office hour regime, whereas operators typically worked in shifts. It was no surprise then that our selection examination was very popular and well-attended. We appointed the one with the best score at the examination and the best overall track record as an operator. It was the logical thing to do but fundamentally wrong.

What I did was take someone out of the value chain who was really good at making quality parts, and as such, added value to the parts. Now I let him do non-value-added work, controlling others. For that, he was paid more and had better working conditions. How wrong can you be if total quality is your proclaimed final objective? This is all with the best intentions, and to improve quality by strengthening the quality department.

But the quality department does not make quality, everyone within the value chain does or does not.

The people who do not have the word, *quality*, in their title make the difference. So, if we want quality and quality knowledge to be of service to the organisation, we need to spread our knowledge, install continual improvement in all aspects of the business, and happily retire with the good feeling of a job well done.

I can reassure quality professionals that getting there will take some time, so there is no reason to panic. Besides, there will always be a lot of work to keep the organisation compliant.

But beyond compliance, where quality starts, an organisation will only be successful if it embeds quality into the value chain.

If we are not purposely and in a structured way, working towards our redundancy, there is the possibility that we will find ourselves redundant if the rest of the organisation no longer sees any added value in what we do.

That would really be a shame, especially because our knowledge can, and should really play a major part in helping organisations and societies become better and more sustainable. The profession and the title do not matter; it is the widespread application of the knowledge that will make the difference.

With the possibility of reaching the absolute essence of quality, our true and only worthwhile goal: making life better for all.

ABBREVIATIONS

AI   : Artificial Intelligence
CEO : Chief Executive Officer
COP : Conference of the Parties
EOQ : European Organisation for Quality
IPCC : Intergovernmental Panel on Climate
         Change
KPIs : Key Performance Indicators
PPM : Parts Per Million
SDGs: Sustainable Development Goals
SPC : Statistical Process Control
UN   : United Nations
US   : United States of America
VCK : Vlaams Centrum voor Kwaliteitszorg
         [the Flemish Quality Management
          Centre, currently known as Xelyo]

ACKNOWLEDGEMENTS

Writing is a lonely activity, but what you write is the result of the interactions you have with many other people. Their stories, their ideas and their experiences have all influenced the writer in some way and have, even unknowingly, contributed to the final outcome.

So I want to thank all the people that I have met during my career in quality, and of which several have become friends. This book would not have come to light without you.

Thanks also to my editor, Kola, for his patience with a stubborn and difficult author.

A special thanks to Els, my wife, for creating the wonderful book cover. And most of all for being able to live with that stubborn and difficult author/person.

ABOUT THE AUTHOR

Willy Vandenbrande was born in 1955 in Brugge, Belgium in a working class family. He was the first and only child of a family of six to attend university. After his engineering studies, he worked as a university research assistant and a project engineer. Later on, he became responsible for a heat treatment plant, as part of a larger company. A couple of years later, he entered the world of quality management, when he became the total quality manager of that company.

After that, Willy entered the consulting world as a quality management consultant, the largest part of his working career.

After 35 years in consulting, he retired in 2022. However, he has stayed active as a writer and presenter. He is a well-liked speaker at international quality conferences, where, amongst other things, he challenges some established norms. As shown in this book, his attention is firmly focused on the impact of quality on sustainability.

Recently he started a new company called "Quality for Nature." This organisation handles his speaking and writing activities. All profits made will be invested in ecosystem restoration projects.

www.ingramcontent.com/pod-product-compliance
Lightning Source LLC
Chambersburg PA
CBHW021925190326
41519CB00009B/910